THE ANNOTATED SHAKESPEARE

Richard III

William Shakespeare

Edited, fully annotated, and introduced by Burton Raffel

With an essay by Harold Bloom

THE ANNOTATED SHAKESPEARE

Yale University Press · *New Haven and London*

Designed by Rebecca Gibb.
Set in Bembo type by The Composing Room of Michigan, Inc.
Printed in the United States of America by R. R. Donnelley & Sons.

Library of Congress Cataloging-in-Publication Data
Shakespeare, William, 1564–1616.
Richard III / William Shakespeare ; edited, fully annotated,
and introduced by Burton Raffel; with an essay by Harold Bloom.
p.   cm. — (The annotated Shakespeare)
ISBN 978-0-300-12202-2 (paperbound)
1. Richard III, King of England, 1452–1485—Drama.
2. Great Britain—History—Richard III, 1483–1485—Drama.
I. Raffel, Burton.   II. Bloom, Harold.   III. Title.
PR2821.A2R34   2008
822.3'3—dc22
2007036416

A catalogue record for this book is available from the British Library.

10 9 8 7 6 5 4 3 2 1

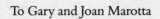

To Gary and Joan Marotta

CONTENTS

*R*ichard III can be singularly difficult going, densely strewn with historically produced linguistic prickles. Here is old Queen Margaret, summing up her long catalogue of injuries and grief:

> Bear with me. I am hungry for revenge,
> And now I cloy me with beholding it.
> Thy Edward he is dead, that stabbed my Edward,
> The other Edward dead, to quit my Edward.
> Young York, he is but boot, because both they
> Matched not the high perfection of my loss.
> Thy Clarence he is dead, that stabbed my Edward,
> And the beholders of this frantic play –
> Th'adulterate Hastings, Rivers, Vaughan, Grey –
> Untimely smothered in their dusky graves.
> Richard yet lives, hell's black intelligencer,
> Only reserved their factor to buy souls
> And send them thither. But at hand, at hand,
> Ensues his piteous and unpitied end,
> Earth gapes, hell burns, fiends roar, saints pray.

This was perfectly understandable, we must assume, to the mostly very average persons who paid to watch Elizabethan plays. But though much remains clear, who today can make full or entirely comfortable sense of it? In this very fully annotated edition, I therefore present this passage, not in the bare form quoted above, but thoroughly supported by bottom-of-the-page notes:

> Bear with me. I am hungry for revenge,
> And now I cloy[1] me with beholding it.
> Thy Edward he is dead, that stabbed my Edward,
> The other Edward dead, to quit my Edward.
> Young York, he is but boot,[2] because both they[3]
> Matched not the high perfection of my loss.
> Thy Clarence he is dead, that stabbed my Edward,
> And the beholders of this frantic play[4] –
> Th'adulterate[5] Hastings, Rivers, Vaughan, Grey –
> Untimely smothered[6] in their dusky graves.
> Richard yet lives, hell's black intelligencer,[7]
> Only reserved[8] their[9] factor to buy souls
> And send them thither. But at hand,[10] at hand,
> Ensues[11] his piteous and unpitied end
> Earth gapes, hell burns, fiends roar, saints pray.

1 overload, surfeit
2 something tossed in, an addition of no particular weight or significance
3 both they = the two sons of Edward IV
4 action, live show
5 adulterous
6 silenced, suppressed, covered
7 spy, agent
8 kept in employment/alive
9 i.e., Hell's
10 at hand = close by
11 follows, pursues

Without full explanation of words that have over the years shifted in meaning, and usages that have been altered, neither the modern reader nor the modern listener is likely to be equipped for anything like full comprehension.

I believe annotations of this sort create the necessary bridges, from Shakespeare's four-centuries-old English across to ours. Some readers, to be sure, will be able to comprehend unusual, historically different meanings without any glosses. Those not familiar with the modern meaning of particular words will easily find clear, simple definitions in any modern dictionary. But most readers are not likely to understand Shakespeare's intended meaning, absent such glosses as I here offer.

The last Renaissance text of the play is the 1623 *Folio,* which I have here followed. But see *This Text,* below.

My annotation practices have followed the same principles used in *The Annotated Milton,* published in 1999, and in my annotated editions of *Hamlet,* published (as the initial volume in this series) in 2003, *Romeo and Juliet* (published in 2004), and subsequent volumes in this series. Classroom experience has validated these editions. Classes of mixed upper-level undergraduates and graduate students have more quickly and thoroughly transcended language barriers than ever before. This allows the teacher, or a general reader without a teacher, to move more promptly and confidently to the nonlinguistic matters that have made Shakespeare and Milton great and important poets.

It is the inevitable forces of linguistic change, operant in all living tongues, which have inevitably created such wide degrees of obstacles to ready comprehension—not only sharply different meanings, but subtle, partial shifts in meaning that allow us to think we understand when, alas, we do not. Speakers of related languages like Dutch and German also experience this shifting of the linguistic ground. Like early Modern English (ca. 1600) and the Modern English now current, those languages are too close for those who know only one language, and not the other, to be readily able always to recognize what they correctly understand and what they do not. When, for example, a speaker of Dutch says, "Men kofer is kapot," a speaker of German will know that something belonging to the Dutchman is broken ("kapot" = "kaputt" in German, and "men" = "mein"). But without more linguistic awareness than the average person is apt to have, the German speaker will not identify "kofer" ("trunk" in Dutch) with "Körper"—a modern German word meaning "physique, build, body." The closest word to "kofer" in modern German, indeed, is "Scrankkoffer," which is too large a leap for ready comprehension. Speakers of different Romance languages (French, Spanish, Italian), and all other related but not identical tongues, all experience these difficulties, as well as the difficulty of understanding a text written in their own language five, or six, or seven hundred years earlier. Shakespeare's English is not yet so old that it requires, like many historical texts in French and German, or like Old English texts—for example, *Beowulf*—a modern translation. Much poetry evaporates in translation: language is immensely particular. The sheer *sound* of Dante in thirteenth-century Italian is profoundly worth preserving. So too is the sound of Shakespeare.

I have annotated prosody (metrics) only when it seemed truly necessary or particularly helpful. Readers should have no problem with the silent "e" in past participles (loved, returned, missed). Except in the few instances where modern usage syllabifies the "e," whenever an "e" in Shakespeare is *not* silent, it is marked "è." The notation used for prosody, which is also used in the explanation of Elizabethan pronunciation, follows the extremely simple form of my *From Stress to Stress: An Autobiography of English Prosody* (see "Further Reading," near the end of this book). Syllables with metrical stress are capitalized; all other syllables are in lowercase letters. I have managed to employ normalized Elizabethan spellings, in most indications of pronunciation, but I have sometimes been obliged to deviate, in the higher interest of being understood.

I have annotated, as well, a limited number of such other matters, sometimes of interpretation, sometimes of general or historical relevance, as have seemed to me seriously worthy of inclusion. These annotations have been most carefully restricted: this is not intended to be a book of literary commentary. It is for that reason that the glossing of metaphors has been severely restricted. There is almost literally no end to discussion and/or analysis of metaphor, especially in Shakespeare. To yield to temptation might well be to double or triple the size of this book—and would also change it from a historically oriented language guide to a work of an unsteadily mixed nature. In the process, I believe, neither language nor literature would be well or clearly served.

Where it seemed useful, and not obstructive of important textual matters, I have modernized spelling, including capitalization. Spelling is not on the whole a basic issue, but punctuation and lineation must be given high respect. The Folio (which is the sole source of our text) uses few exclamation marks or semicolons, which is to be sure a matter of the conventions of a very different era. Still, our modern preferences cannot be lightly substituted for what is, after a fashion, the closest thing to a Shakespeare manuscript we are likely ever to have. We do not know whether these particular seventeenth-century printers, like most of that time, were responsible for question marks, commas, periods, and, especially, all-purpose colons, or whether these particular printers tried to follow their handwritten sources. Nor do we know if those sources, or what part thereof, might have been in Shakespeare's own hand. But in spite of these equivocations and uncertainties, it remains true that, to a very considerable extent, punctuation tends to result from just how the mind responsible for that punctuating *hears* the text. And twenty-first-century minds have no business, in such matters, overruling seventeenth-century ones. Whoever the compositors were, they were more or less Shakespeare's contemporaries, and we are not.

Accordingly, when the original printed text uses a comma, we are being signaled that *they* (whoever "they" were) heard the text, not coming to a syntactic stop, but continuing to some later stopping point. To replace commas with editorial periods is thus risky and on the whole an undesirable practice. (The dramatic action of a tragedy, to be sure, may require us, for twenty-first-century readers, to highlight what four-hundred-year-old punctuation standards may not make clear—and may even, at times, misrepresent.)

When the printed text has a colon, what we are being signaled is that *they* heard a syntactic stop—though not necessarily or even usually the particular kind of syntactic stop we associate, today, with the colon. It is therefore inappropriate to substitute editorial commas for original colons. It is also inappropriate to employ editorial colons when *their* syntactic usage of colons does not match ours. In general, the closest thing to *their* syntactic sense of the colon is our (and their) period.

The printed interrogation (question) marks, too, merit extremely respectful handling. In particular, editorial exclamation marks should very rarely be substituted for interrogation marks.

It follows from these considerations that the movement and sometimes the meaning of what we must take to be Shakespeare's *play* will at times be different, depending on whose punctuation we follow, *theirs* or our own. I have tried, here, to use the printed seventeenth-century text as a guide to both *hearing* and *understanding* what Shakespeare wrote.

Since the original printed texts (there not being, as there never are for Shakespeare, any surviving manuscripts) are frequently careless as well as self-contradictory, I have been relatively free with the wording of stage directions—and in some cases have added brief directions, to indicate who is speaking to whom. I have made no emendations; I have necessarily been obliged to make choices. Textual decisions have been annotated when the differences between or among the original printed texts seem either marked or of unusual interest.

In the interests of compactness and brevity, I have employed in my annotations (as consistently as I am able) a number of stylistic and typographical devices:

- The annotation of a single word does not repeat that word

- The annotation of more than one word repeats the words being annotated, which are followed by an equals sign and then by the annotation; the footnote number in the text is placed after the last of the words being annotated

- In annotations of a single word, alternative meanings are usually separated by commas; if there are distinctly different ranges of meaning, the annotations are separated by arabic numerals inside parentheses—(1), (2), and so on; in more complexly worded annotations, alternative meanings expressed by a single word are linked by a forward slash, or solidus: /

- Explanations of textual meaning are not in parentheses; comments about textual meaning are

- Except for proper nouns, the word at the beginning of all annotations is in lower case

- Uncertainties are followed by a question mark, set in parentheses: (?)

- When particularly relevant, "translations" into twenty-first-century English have been added, in parentheses

- Annotations of repeated words are *not* repeated. Explanations of the *first* instance of such common words are followed by the sign ★. Readers may easily track down the first annotation, using the brief Finding List at the back of the book. Words with entirely separate meanings are annotated *only* for meanings no longer current in Modern English.

The most important typographical device here employed is the sign ★ placed after the first (and only) annotation of words and phrases occurring more than once. There is an alphabetically arranged listing of such words and phrases in the Finding List at the back of the book. The Finding List contains no annotations but simply gives the words or phrases themselves and the numbers of the relevant act, the scene within that act, and the foot-note number within that scene for the word's first occurrence.

This Text

All of Shakespeare's plays have textual uncertainties, but some of the texts are more uncertain than others. *Richard III* is arguably the most confused of all. There are two primary texts, the First Quarto (1597) and the Folio (1623).[12] The seven successor quarto editions, printed one from the next (and from all those before), are of minimal importance. I have not ignored them, but neither have I much followed them.

It has been argued that the First Quarto, because it is the earliest, is thus the closest to the actual performing text of Shakespeare's play. On its face a reasonable assumption, this argument is refuted by the First Quarto's extraordinary number and range of typographical errors (many rendering the text incomprehensible). In the course of correcting the First Quarto, and its descendants, the Folio text inevitably introduces new errors. Early printing was an inherently error-producing process. On the whole, however, the Folio is clearly a "better" text. If it sometimes cuts rather too much out of the First Quarto, mostly its excisions and alterations have been intelligently and sensitively made, and ill-advised cuts can be and are here (as in most modern editions they are) restored. And considering the authority of those friends and associates of the playwright who produced the Folio, the general superiority of that text is hardly surprising. The punctuation of the Folio is very much better—but though it is a significant mark of care and good sense, punctuation alone does not make a good text. And the Folio is plainly not entirely a "good" text.

With two primary texts, neither wholly satisfactory, an editor cannot choose a "copy text"—that is, a unitary text with clear authority—and simply follow wherever it goes. One must constantly work back and forth, picking and choosing as best one can. I have kept the two primary texts constantly in front of me, and done my best to choose correctly—or at least sensibly. The task is of course impossible: twenty-first century editors are no more Shakespeare than was/were the compositor(s) of the First Quarto or the compositor(s) and editors of the Folio. The discussion of my editorial procedures, just above, is I think a reasonable guide to how my editing has been accomplished.

INTRODUCTION

*R*ichard III was probably written in 1591–1592; the exact date is uncertain. Francis Meres listed it, in 1592, as one of the up-and-coming young playwright's works. Nor do we have a certain date for the play's first performance or even for just which acting company it had been composed. The first of a string of Quarto publications (eight in all) appeared in 1597, making it a reasonable assumption that the play was very well received. But the first more than merely bibliographical reference to *Richard III,* in surviving documents, does not come until 1602.

There is a strong undercurrent of uncertainty, too, in much of modern critical commentary. Harold C. Goddard's fine survey of Shakespeare's work, for example, deals with the play in terms of insistently polarized judgments. "*Richard III,* from beginning to end, is marked by juvenility and genius. . . . [It] is one thing if considered an early play . . . [but] another and more impressive one when taken as the climax and conclusion of the eight English History Plays. . . . Though it is often closer to melodrama than to tragedy, and has more rhetoric and eloquence than poetry, more breadth than depth of characterization, all through it there are hints and gleams of the highest things . . . and its general moral intention and upshot are as sound as those of the later Trag-edies. . . . In spite of its immaturities, *Richard III* remains one of the most powerful presentations of the idea of nemesis in any lit-erature."[1] It would be difficult to be more conclusively inconclu-sive. Were this an isolated reaction, it might well point to a prob-lem in critical perception, an inability to place the play in a clear-enough perspective that the commentator can make firm and confident evaluations.

But this is not simply an isolated reaction. Theodore Weiss, af-ter acknowledging the dramaturgical innovations of *Richard III*—its intense dramatic reorganization of historical information and its use of the historical main figure as "playwright, director, chief actor, principal member of the vast audience he has captivated, and most discerning critic"—remarks that "whatever the play may lack in subtlety and depth, or in delicate poetry, . . . it com-pensates for in its unabating power, in its sudden thunderous strokes, and in the sardonic, ruthless élan of Richard." Weiss con-cludes an analysis much longer and detailed than Goddard's with a series of similarly polarized assertions: "At the same time we must realize that in his very triumph of excess Richard is serving, unknown to himself, an end much greater than his own. . . . [This] is indeed a kind of satyr play. . . . Like a Dionysian satyr, rending all in his riotous path, Richard in the end . . . must be torn to pieces, sacrificed in the way he has sacrificed others."[2]

"Richard is a brilliant villain," Mark Van Doren's analysis be-gins. "The conduct of the drama is simple and every effect is pur-sued to the extreme . . ." Yet this sentence continues, asserting that "the play is long and sometimes laborious; but the total achieve-ment has its magnificence." Such distinctly left-handed praise is put aside for a time, there being of course much of a positive nature to be said. But the final paragraph of Van Doren's discussion flatly reasserts critical ambivalence: "With all this there is no refinement in Richard's character viewed as a whole. He is called the devil as often as Iago is . . . [and] partakes of . . . terrors no less than Macbeth. . . . Yet the effect remains external. . . . Shakespeare has not yet discovered the secret of a true success in fables of this kind."[3]

Robert Ornstein also begins with firm praise. "A stunning success in Shakespeare's time, *Richard III* has been a favorite of succeeding generations of actors and audiences. Like *Hamlet,* it has never failed to hold the stage because it is superbly theatrical." But soon enough, ambivalence intrudes (as it does throughout his study of the history plays, the first page of which asks "why Shakespeare seems at times less certain a craftsman in this genre than in his comedies and tragedies"). "Although the sense of the past evoked in the rhetoric of the choric and ritual scenes is necessary to the play, it is a burden on modern audiences. . . . The portrayal of Richard's loss of control in the coronation scene is masterful. Thereafter, his uncertainties grow repetitious and his hesitations undramatic. . . . The pageant of ghosts seems an appropriately archaic device with which to recapitulate the past; the attempt to make Richard bear witness against himself is less successful."[4]

Matthew H. Wikander clearly states that "*Richard III* poses special problems. . . . [Richard's] affinities with the ever-popular Vice of [the] morality [play] tradition . . . delights the audience . . . [but] his loss of zest upon gaining the kingship loses the audience's sympathy. The theatrical experience of the play challenges the historical lesson: where the chroniclers celebrate the coming of Richmond [Henry VII] as an end to civil unrest, Shakespeare leaves the audience flat."[5]

But Peter Saccio provides, I think, the key to a steadier perspective: "The Tudor imagination revelled in Richard III."[6] As Tom F. Driver neatly puts the matter: "Here, as elsewhere, Shakespeare shows no fear of a mixture of styles. The language ranges from the lofty and rhetorical, in Richmond's addresses, to the mundane and comic in the quiverings of the Second Murderer. Between these extremes lies the whimsical, artificial, self-directed speech of Richard. In *Richard III,* language and structure united to create a form that expresses an action essentially temporal and historical in conception. Shakespeare looks for the larger, universal-historical action within which the smaller, transient one may be understood. . . . In *Richard III* one moves in an atmosphere of memory, decision, and expectation."[7] All of which, it seems to me, is yet another way of affirming that, in trying to understand and evaluate the major work of so magnificent a writer as Shakespeare, we must allow what he has written to give us the basic clues. If we allow ourselves to be overly much guided by what we ourselves bring to such an understanding and evaluation, we are likely to subordinate Shakespeare's approach to our own. Surely, we must know ourselves; we too are important and valued. But understanding Shakespeare cannot and must not be confused with, and subordinated to, an understanding of ourselves. To paraphrase George Orwell's *Animal Farm,* some understandings understand more than others.

What we actually find in *Richard III* is a masterfully spread-out tapestry—certainly a "history" play but, more important, a powerfully literary reimagining of the sudden rise to the throne and brief reign of the last Lancastrian king. Shakespeare weaves his tale onto a large and yet wonderfully well-contained frame, deploying a wide range of theatrical devices with consummate, deft ease and brilliantly evocative language.

> Now is the winter of our discontent
> Made glorious summer by this son of York,
> And all the clouds that loured upon our house
> In the deep bosom of the ocean buried.
>
> (1.1.1–4)

Still no more than the Duke of Gloucester, as the play opens, Richard is alone on the stage as he speaks these first words of the play. To begin with such grandly sweeping lines, beautifully melding seasonal metaphors with the changing of political and dynastic fortunes, surely announces *poetic* drama of the highest order. To declare that this is a play lacking in "delicate poetry," a play that features "more rhetoric and eloquence than poetry," seems on the face of it implausible. *Richard III* is, as I have indicated, an amalgam of diverse dramatic elements; it is a fairly "early" play (though mere chronology is no more relevant to Shakespeare's career than it is to Mozart's or Picasso's); and it is profoundly stormy, its stark and bitter moments placed side by side with witty ones. Intensely dramatic struggles are mixed with burlesque, courage with cowardice, corruption with repentance. Does Shakespeare successfully blend the play's far-flung components? Read *it*—not its critics—and you will find that the answer can only be an emphatic affirmative.

> But I, that am not shaped for sportive tricks,
> Nor made to court an amorous looking-glass –

I, that am rudely stamped, and want love's majesty

To strut before a wanton ambling nymph –

I, that am curtailed of this fair proportion,

Cheated of feature by dissembling nature,

Deformed, unfinished, sent before my time

Into this breathing world, scarce half made up

(And that so lamely and unfashionable

That dogs bark at me as I halt by them),

Why, I, in this weak piping time of peace,

Have no delight to pass away the time,

Unless to see my shadow in the sun

And descant on mine own deformity.

$$(1.1.5-18)$$

Richard's play-opening speech thus swings the focus away from the triumphs of his family and plainly, bluntly on himself. He speaks in and for the play; he *is* to a large extent the play. Richard's biting self-portrait not only does not lack depth of characterization, it is magnificently, sonorously a prelude to what he prefigures as a violent, jarring overturn of "glorious summer." Shakespeare's audience, of course, had an immediacy of foreknowledge that we, more than four centuries later, necessarily lack. They "reveled" in the character and the tale of Richard, as Americans still tell and retell the assassination of John F. Kennedy, and even the assassination of Abraham Lincoln. But the Greek audiences of Aeschylus, Sophocles, and Euripides also knew the tales their playwrights were telling. The power of these Greek retellings was exactly the power of all great reimaginings, which do not depend on mere plot suspense.

And still alone on stage, still in the play's initial moments,

Richard continues—far more subtly than either he or the play has been given credit for—to move forward with the weaving of Shakespeare's complex tapestry:

> And therefore, since I cannot prove a lover,
> To entertain these fair well-spoken days
> I am determined to prove a villain.

(I.I.19–21)

Richard brought onto the Elizabethan stage his well-established reputation as a smoothly deceptive, endlessly shifting, and self-serving character, relentlessly ambitious and, despite his unending flow of verbal disguises, ruthlessly and single-mindedly cruel. The audience knew too much about him to believe that what would follow this apparently flippant announcement, "I am determined to prove a villain," would be a mere melodramatic joke, a sardonic Senecan blood-romp. We need to keep strictly in mind the nature of the man who speaks these words. Is there in all of Shakespeare (or indeed in all the literature of the world) anyone whose words are less trustworthy than Richard's? His character, as Shakespeare presents him, has often, and justly, been compared to that of Iago. Yet Iago represents pure, pointless evil. He *says* he wants power, he wants rank, he wants wealth. But whatever he gets is never enough, can never be enough. Richard's evil, no less perfect and surely no less intense, is in truth performed for specific purposes. Like the madly power- and wealth-hungry character in *Kind Hearts and Coronets,* a man who one by one kills everyone standing in the way of his lust for power and wealth, Richard not only disposes of all those in his way—men, women, and children—but also disposes of those he has made use of and no longer needs. This is not psychotic evil but simple everyday evil carried out on a royal plain. Iago has trouble actually killing anyone; he is a very bad soldier. Richard can and does kill right and left, and indeed goes down to his death still powerfully swinging a sword. "A horse, a horse, my kingdom for a horse!" Iago dies sullenly and silently; Richard dies as he has lived, vociferously and aggressively. We do not have to choose between the evil Iago and Richard both represent, but we do need to distinguish one from the other.

Richard III makes use of a large cast—men, women, and children—and offers characterizations as profoundly three-dimensional as we have any right to expect from a drama based on then familiar historical events. (How much leeway, in these matters, would a playwright have, dealing with George Washington, the Duke of Wellington, or the Marquis de Lafayette?) Richard, who until the fifth and last act totally dominates the stage, is seen interacting with two children, almost thirty adult men, and four adult women. All the many male roles remain subordinate, supporting rather than controlling the play's action. Far from being standardized, flat characterizations, each male appears clearly his own man, and each is given fine, often stirringly beautiful poetry.

The first supporting male we see is George, Duke of Clarence, Richard's wastrel, greedy, traitorous older brother. This aging playboy immediately characterizes himself:

Richard   Brother, good day. What means this armèd guard
    That waits upon your Grace?
Clarence   His Majesty,
    Tend'ring my person's safety, hath appointed
    This conduct to convey me to the Tower.

Gloucester Upon what cause?

Clarence   Because my name is George.

                                    (1.1.43–47)

But there his character presents far more than this unsurprising
sardonic wit. Imprisoned in the Tower of London, rightly fearful,
he relates to his jailer a tormenting dream, in which he is acci-
dentally thrown

> Into the tumbling billows of the main.
> O Lord, methought what pain it was to drown,
> What dreadful noise of waters in mine ears!
> What sights of ugly death within mine eyes.
> Methoughts I saw a thousand fearful wracks,
> A thousand men that fishes gnawed upon,
> Wedges of gold, great anchors, heaps of pearl,
> Inestimable stones, unvalued jewels,
> All scattered in the bottom of the sea.
> Some lay in dead men's skulls, and in those holes
> Where eyes did once inhabit, there were crept,
> As 'twere in scorn of eyes, reflecting gems,
> Which wooed the slimy bottom of the deep,
> And mocked the dead bones that lay scattered by.
>
>   (1.4.20–33)

Tonally very like Shakespeare's deeply poetical *The Tempest,* this
begins a clear, carefully elaborated revelation of Clarence's shaken
soul, ending with a poignant, almost childlike plea to the jailer,
"Keeper, I prithee sit by me a while. / My soul is heavy, and I fain
would sleep" (lines 73–74). Soon the murderers arrive—and
what we have already seen of Clarence's tremulous state prepares

us for, and fully justifies his words to them: "Take heed. For he [God] holds vengeance in his hand, / To hurl upon their heads that break his law" (lines 185–186).

The smug complacency of Hastings, carried in lines of confidently, evenly modulated verse, emerges at once. Richard asks, "How hath your lordship brooked imprisonment?" and Hastings proclaims:

> With patience (noble lord) as prisoners must.
> But I shall live (my lord) to give them thanks
> That were the cause of my imprisonment.
>
> (1.1.128–130)

Shakespeare does not casually pen three consecutive lines of such completely regular iambic pentameter. As I have written elsewhere, "Words and prosody thus work together . . . to create an admittedly small but nevertheless distinct and by no means negligible effect. Why else, indeed, would Shakespeare have bothered to create it? His ear dictated it precisely because his ear, like his audience's ears, *could* detect it, as all their respective ears were and had been in the habit of doing. These kinds of prosodic signals are plainly deliberate, and they just as plainly work."[8] When Hastings chastises Queen Margaret, in act 1, scene 3, both the righteousness and the triteness of his complacency, are neatly displayed, in a mere two lines: "False-boding woman, end thy frantic curse, / Lest to thy harm thou move our patience" (lines 246–247). Hastings' self-deceived sense of security is, as one might expect, tenaciously set in place; his is not a flexible mind:

> But I shall laugh at this a twelvemonth hence,
> That they who brought me in my master's hate
> I live to look upon their tragedy.

Well Catesby, ere a fortnight make me older,
I'll send some packing that yet think not on it.

(3.2.56–60)

Even when Stanley seriously questions his confidence, Hastings
remains supremely self-assured:

My lord, I hold my life as dear as yours,
And never in my days, I do protest,
Was it so precious to me as 'tis now.
Think you, but that I know our state secure,
I would be so triumphant as I am?

(3.2.76–80)

Indeed, Hastings is utterly unshakeable until moments before his
downfall. Richard is in a remarkably good mood, he explains to
his less-perceptive colleagues. And how does he know? Why, one
has only to look at him, he declares:

I think there's never a man in Christendom
Can lesser hide his love, or hate, than he,
For by his face straight shall you know his heart.

(3.4.51–53)

Even on his way to his execution, Hastings' mind seems wretch-
edly single-faceted:

O bloody Richard! Miserable England,
I prophesy the fearful'st time to thee
That ever wretched age hath looked upon.
Come, lead me to the block, bear him my head.
They smile at me, who shortly shall be dead.

(3.4.103–107)

We do not need to march through the more than two dozen male roles, here. Some are slighter than others; some are more memorable than others. But all are superbly delineated, and all have sharply etched poetry to speak.

Yet the main bloc of resistance to Richard's taking the crown is represented, not by any of the male characters, singly or in groupings, but by the four royal women, who often speak as a group (a "chorus")—though Anne is replaced, toward the end of the play, by Elizabeth. This all-female chorus is echoed, confirmed, and strengthened by the choral voices of ghosts—males, females, and children—which appear in act 5. (There are additional choric aspects to the elaborate question-and-answer exchanges between Richard and Anne, in act 1, scene 2, and Richard and Elizabeth, in act 4, scene 4.) None of the women, to be sure, is able to mount the kind of armed opposition that Margaret, younger and then far more powerful, once mounted against Richard's father and his associated Yorkists. They are queenly, and one (the Duchess of York) is Richard's mother, but they are limited not only by age (Margaret) and, all four of them, by the gender boundaries of late medieval society, but also, in the cases of Anne and Elizabeth, by the kind of weakness of spirit to which the relatively stolid Duchess of York is immune. Collectively and individually, they provide an insistent, irrepressible morality that, bit by bit, becomes echoed and supplemented by the moral realizations forced on many of the male characters. And in the end, for this drama is in many ways an evocation of the old morality plays, the path is prepared for the destruction of Richard and the triumphant return of a "true" and virtuous king. On her first appearance, in act 1, scene 2, Anne signals the need for this moral reawakening, both by urging her knightly attendants to stand up to Richard and by her own fierce attack: "What, do you tremble? Are you all afraid?" she scolds, after which she forgives them and begins her direct assault on Richard. "Alas, I blame you not, for you are mortal, / And mortal eyes cannot endure the devil. / Avaunt, thou dreadful minister of hell!" (lines 43–46). (When he has won her over, Richard is half amazed at his cynically motivated success; his exclamation is poetry of the highest order: "Was ever woman in this humor wooed? / Was ever woman in this humor won?" (lines 230–231).

Margaret, old and twisted, makes herself a one-voice chorus, in the next scene, standing to the side of the stage and muttering witchlike imprecations:

> Out, devil! . . .
> Thou killed my husband Henry in the Tower,
> And Edward, my poor son, at Tewkesbury.
>
> (1.3.117–119)

She finally steps forward and attacks, not only Richard, but all the others present:

> Hear me, you wrangling pirates, that fall out
> In sharing that which you have pilled from me!
> Which of you trembles not that looks on me?
>
> (1.3.157–159)

Margaret attacks them all, but Richard most vehemently. They counterattack, but her curses become, indeed, exactly what she proclaims them, prophecies that turn to facts:

> What, dost thou scorn me for my gentle counsel,
> And soothe the devil that I warn thee from?

O but remember this another day,
When he shall split thy very heart with sorrow,
And say poor Margaret was a prophetess!
Live each of you the subjects to his hate,
And he to yours, and all of you to God's!

(1.3.296–302)

After the death of Edward IV, his widowed queen, Elizabeth, and
his mother, the Duchess of York, together with Edward's children, sound a profoundly mournful chorus:

Elizabeth   Give me no help in lamentation,
    I am not barren to bring forth complaints.
    All springs reduce their currents to mine eyes,
    That I, being governed by the watery moon,
    May send forth plenteous tears to drown the world!
    Ah, for my husband, for my dear Lord Edward!
Children   Ah, for our father, for our dear Lord Clarence!
Duchess of York Alas for both, both mine, Edward and Clarence!
Elizabeth   What stay had I but Edward, and he's gone.
Children   What stay had we but Clarence? And he's gone.
Duchess of York What stays had I but they? And they are gone.
Elizabeth   Was never widow had so dear a loss!
Children   Were never orphans had so dear a loss!
Duchess of York Was never mother had so dear a loss!
    Alas, I am the mother of these griefs,
    Their woes are parceled, mine are general.
    She for an Edward weeps, and so do I.
    I for a Clarence weep, so doth not she.
    These babes for Clarence weep, and so do I.
    I for an Edward weep, so do not they.

Alas! You three, on me threefold distressed,
Pour all your tears, I am your sorrow's nurse,
And I will pamper it with lamentation.

(2.2.66–88)

This funereal chorus resonates with both Anne's and Margaret's denunciations. We do not hear a chorus again until act 4, but the road leading to it has been eloquently strewn with misery:

Elizabeth (*to Anne*) Poor heart adieu, I pity thy
complaining.
Anne No more than from my soul I mourn for yours.
Elizabeth Farewell, thou woeful welcomer of glory.
Anne Adieu, poor soul, that tak'st thy leave of it.
Duchess of York (*to Dorset*) Go thou to Richmond, and good
fortune guide thee.
(*to Anne*) Go thou to Richard, and good angels guard thee.
(*to Elizabeth*) Go thou to sanctuary, and good thoughts possess
thee.
I to my grave, where peace and rest lie with me.

(4.1.87–94)

By act 4, scene 4, Anne is dead; the passionate chorus is composed of Margaret (at first to one side and heard by the audience but not by the other two women), Elizabeth, and the Duchess of York:

Elizabeth Ah my poor princes! Ah my tender babes!
My unblown flowers, new-appearing sweets!
If yet your gentle souls fly in the air
And be not fixed in doom perpetual,
Hover about me with your airy wings
And hear your mother's lamentation!

Margaret   (*aside*) Hover about her, say that right for right
  Hath dimmed your infant morn to agèd night.
Duchess of York So many miseries have crazed my voice
  That my woe-wearied tongue is mute and dumb.
  Edward Plantagenet, why art thou dead?
Margaret   (*aside*) Plantagenet doth quit Plantagenet.
  Edward for Edward pays a dying debt.
Elizabeth   Wilt thou, O God, fly from such gentle lambs,
  And throw them in the entrails of the wolf?
  When didst thou sleep when such a deed was done?
Margaret   (*aside*) When holy Harry died, and my sweet son.
Duchess of York Dead life, blind sight, poor mortal living ghost,
  Woe's scene, world's shame, grave's due by life usurped,
  Brief abstract and record of tedious days,
  Rest thy unrest on England's lawful earth
  (*sitting*) Unlawfully made drunk with innocent blood.
Elizabeth   Ah that thou wouldst as soon afford a grave
  As thou canst yield a melancholy seat!
  Then would I hide my bones, not rest them here.
  Ah who hath any cause to mourn but we?

SITTING DOWN BY HER

Margaret   (*coming forward*) If ancient sorrow be most
  reverend,
  Give mine the benefit of seigniory,
  And let my griefs frown on the upper hand.
  (*sitting with them*) If sorrow can admit society,
  Tell o'er your woes again by viewing mine.
  I had an Edward, till a Richard killed him.

I had a husband, till a Richard killed him.

Thou hadst an Edward, till a Richard killed him.

Thou hadst a Richard, till a Richard killed him.

Duchess of York I had a Richard too, and thou didst kill him.

I had a Rutland too, thou holp'st to kill him.

Margaret   Thou hadst a Clarence too, and Richard

killed him.

From forth the kennel of thy womb hath crept

A hell-hound that doth hunt us all to death.

That dog, that had his teeth before his eyes,

To worry lambs and lap their gentle blood,

That foul defacer of God's handiwork,

That excellent grand tyrant of the earth,

That reigns in gallèd eyes of weeping souls,

Thy womb let loose, to chase us to our graves.

(4.4.9–54)

After Margaret leaves, the Duchess of York confronts and in ex-
plicit terms curses her son:

Either thou wilt die, by God's just ordinance,

Ere from this war thou turn a conqueror,

Or I with grief and extreme age shall perish

And never look upon thy face again.

Therefore take with thee my most grievous curse,

Which in the day of battle tire thee more

Than all the complete armor that thou wear'st.

My prayers on the adverse party fight,

And there the little souls of Edward's children

Whisper the spirits of thine enemies

And promise them success and victory.
Bloody thou art, bloody will be thy end.
Shame serves thy life, and doth thy death attend.

(4.4.184–196)

The human chorus has finished; once the ghostly chorus has spoken, Richard is swiftly swept into death.

As fully, intricately, and highly dramatically imagined by Shakespeare, *Richard III* is and has always been a resounding success. But the play is much less successful as history—even in terms of the necessarily limited historical knowledge available to Shakespeare. This is not the place for a detailed critique of Shakespeare's constant manipulation of chronology or his fudging of issues like that of Richard's deformity, both historically unproven and on the face of it, even in this play, totally improbable. How does a man with a withered arm and a lame (or hunched) back fight so courageously and largely triumphantly as, at the end of act 5, Richard has done? "In spite of his slender physique," says the modern historian Charles Ross, author of the definitive biographical study, "Richard was a tough, hardy and energetic man, who had a proper taste for manly pursuits." His remarkable valor in the battle at Bosworth Field is not a Shakespearean invention. "Richard himself cut down Sir William Brandon, Henry [Richmond]'s standard-bearer. . . . He then engaged and finally overbore Sir John Cheyne, described as a man of outstanding strength and fortitude." Even when the battle was clearly lost, "Richard continued to fight on bravely, 'making way with weapon on every side,' until he was finally overthrown. . . . 'Alone,' says Polydore [a contemporary chronicler], 'he was killed fighting manfully in the press of his enemies.'"[9]

Richmond was, of course, the grandfather of Shakespeare's and England's longtime queen, Elizabeth I. Tudor commentators inevitably presented their dynasty in favorable terms—but Henry VII, though a better king than Edward IV or Richard III, was neither deeply loved nor canonized, as he is in Shakespeare's play. (Nor, as I have indicated, did Henry in fact kill Richard in heroic, God-inspired hand-to-hand combat.) As Ross writes, "Because the more hostile of the Tudor writers, and Shakespeare, chose to select Richard as an object-lesson in villainy and tyranny is no good reason to view him in isolation from the conditions in which he lived. . . . To put Richard . . . into the context of his own violent age is not to make him morally a better man, but at least it makes him more understandable."[10] Other kings, or aspirants to the throne, had been involved in as many proven murders. It seems unlikely that he killed his first wife, Anne, but very likely that he killed the princes in the Tower, though we cannot be certain. We will never know if he was cynical or sincere in his generosity to educational and religious institutions. But other rulers have been praised for less, and their inevitably mixed motivations downplayed or ignored. Quoting another historian's sober assessment, Ross records this evaluation of Richard's brief reign: "In the course of a mere eighteen months, crowded with cares and problems, he laid down a coherent programme of legal enactments, maintained an orderly society, and actively promoted the well-being of his subjects."[11] "As a myth," declares Peter Saccio, "the Tudor Richard is indestructible, nor should one try to destroy him. This demonic jester and archetypical wicked uncle is far too satisfying a creation . . . As history, however, the Tudor Richard is unacceptable."[12] But neither Richmond nor his supporters were angelic. Richard's "crown, taken from a thorn bush, was set on Henry [Richmond]'s head by Lord Stanley, and his naked body, thrown over a horse's back, was sent to Leicester for burial."[13]

Notes

1. Harold C. Goddard, *The Meaning of Shakespeare,* 2 vols. (Chicago: University of Chicago Press, 1951), 1:35, 36, 40.
2. Theodore Weiss, *The Breath of Clowns and Kings: Shakespeare's Early Comedies and Histories* (New York: Atheneum, 1971), 159, 200.
3. Mark Van Doren, *Shakespeare* (New York: Holt, 1939), 19, 26–27.
4. Robert Ornstein, *A Kingdom for a Stage: The Achievement of Shakespeare's History Plays* (Cambridge, Mass.: Harvard University Press, 1972), 62, 64, 75, 78.
5. Matthew H. Wikander, *The Play of Truth and State: Historical Drama from Shakespeare to Brecht* (Baltimore: Johns Hopkins University Press, 1986), 31.
6. Peter Saccio, *Shakespeare's English Kings,* 2nd ed. (Oxford: Oxford University Press, 1997), 157.
7. Tom F. Driver, *The Sense of History in Greek and Shakespearean Drama* (New York: Columbia University Press, 1960), 105.
8. Burton Raffel, "Metrical Dramaturgy in Shakespeare's Earlier Plays," *CEA Critic* 57 (Spring–Summer 1995): 52.
9. Charles Ross, *Richard III* (Berkeley: University of California Press, 1983), 142, 224–225.
10. Ibid., 228–229.
11. Ibid., 189.
12. Saccio, *Shakespeare's English Kings,* 159.
13. Keith Feiling, *A History of England* (New York: McGraw-Hill, 1948), 314.

SOME ESSENTIALS OF THE
SHAKESPEAREAN STAGE

◆───◆

The Stage

- There was no *scenery* (backdrops, flats, and so on).

- Compared to today's elaborate, high-tech productions, the Elizabethan stage had few *on-stage* props. These were mostly handheld: a sword or dagger, a torch or candle, a cup or flask. Larger props, such as furniture, were used sparingly.

- Costumes (some of which were upper-class castoffs, belonging to the individual actors) were elaborate. As in most premodern and very hierarchical societies, clothing was the distinctive mark of who and what a person was.

- What the actors *spoke,* accordingly, contained both the dramatic and narrative material we have come to expect in a theater (or movie house) and (1) the setting, including details of the time of day, the weather, and so on, and (2) the occasion. The *dramaturgy* is thus very different from that of our own time, requiring much more attention to verbal and gestural matters. Strict realism was neither intended nor, under the circumstances, possible.

- There was *no curtain*. Actors entered and left via doors in the back of the stage, behind which was the "tiring-room," where actors put on or changed their costumes.

- In *public theaters* (which were open-air structures), there was no *lighting;* performances could take place only in daylight hours.

- For *private* theaters, located in large halls of aristocratic houses, candlelight illumination was possible.

The Actors

- Actors worked in *professional,* for-profit companies, sometimes organized and owned by other actors, and sometimes by entrepreneurs who could afford to erect or rent the company's building. Public theaters could hold, on average, two thousand playgoers, most of whom viewed and listened while standing. Significant profits could be and were made. Private theaters were smaller, more exclusive.

- There was *no director*. A book-holder / prompter / props manager, standing in the tiring-room behind the backstage doors, worked from a text marked with entrances and exits and notations of any special effects required for that particular script. A few such books have survived. Actors had texts only of their own parts, speeches being cued to a few prior words. There were few and often no rehearsals, in our modern use of the term, though there was often some coaching of individuals. Since Shakespeare's England was largely an oral culture, actors learned their parts rapidly and retained them for years. This was *repertory* theater, repeating popular plays and introducing some new ones each season.

- *Women* were not permitted on the professional stage. Most female roles were acted by *boys;* elderly women were played by grown men.

The Audience

- London's professional theater operated in what might be called a "red-light" district, featuring brothels, restaurants, and the kind of *open-air entertainment* then most popular, like bear-baiting (in which a bear, tied to a stake, was set on by dogs).

- A theater audience, like most of the population of Shakespeare's England, was largely made up of *illiterates.* Being able to read and write, however, had nothing to do with intelligence or concern with language, narrative, and characterization. People attracted to the theater tended to be both extremely verbal and extremely volatile. Actors were sometimes attacked, when the audience was dissatisfied; quarrels and fights were relatively common. Women were regularly in attendance, though no reliable statistics exist.

- Drama did not have the cultural esteem it has in our time, and plays were not regularly printed. Shakespeare's often appeared in book form, but not with any supervision or other involvement on his part. He wrote a good deal of nondramatic poetry as well, yet so far as we know he did not authorize or supervise *any* work of his that appeared in print during his lifetime.

- Playgoers, who had paid good money to see and hear, plainly gave dramatic performances careful, detailed attention. For some closer examination of such matters, see Burton Raffel,

"Who Heard the Rhymes and How: Shakespeare's Dramaturgical Signals," *Oral Tradition* 11 (October 1996): 190–221, and Raffel, "Metrical Dramaturgy in Shakespeare's Earlier Plays," *CEA Critic* 57 (Spring–Summer 1995): 51–65.

Richard III

CHARACTERS (DRAMATIS PERSONAE)

King Edward IV

Edward, Prince of Wales (the King's oldest son)

Richard, Duke of York (the King's younger son)

George, Duke of Clarence (the King's next oldest brother)

Richard, Duke of Gloucester[1] (the King's youngest brother, later King Richard III)

Edward (Clarence's young son)

Henry, Earl of Richmond (later King Henry VIII)

Cardinal Bourchier (Archbishop of Canterbury)

Thomas Rotherham (Archbishop of York)

John Morton (Bishop of Ely)

Duke of Buckingham

Duke of Norfolk (Northumberland)

Earl of Surrey (Norfolk's son*)*

Earl Rivers (Queen Elizabeth's brother, Anthony Woodville)

Marquis[2] *of Dorset* (Queen Elizabeth's son by her prior marriage)

Grey (Queen Elizabeth's son by her prior marriage)

Earl of Oxford

Stanley (Earl of Derby, Count of Richmond)

Hastings (Lord Chamberlain)

Sir Thomas Lovel

Sir Thomas Vaughan

Sir Richard Ratcliff

Sir William Catesby

Sir James Tyrrel

Sir James Blount

Sir Walter Herbert

Sir Robert Brakenbury (in charge of the Tower)

Sir William Brandon

Lord Mayor of London

Tressel, Berkeley (gentlemen attendants on Lady Anne)

Sir Christopher Urswick (a priest)

another priest

Queen Elizabeth (Edward IV's wife)

Queen Margaret (Henry VI's widow)

Duchess of York (mother of Edward IV, Gloucester, and Clarence)

Lady Anne (betrothed [pledged to be married] to Henry VI's son, Edward, Prince of Wales; later, Richard III's wife)

Clarence's young daughter (also named Margaret)

Ghosts of those murdered by Richard III

Lords, attendants, bishops, priests, sheriff, jailer, murderers, scrivener, herald, page, citizens, messengers, soldiers, etc.

1 GLOSSter

2 MARkwiss

Act I

SCENE I

London, A street

ENTER GLOUCESTER[1]

Gloucester Now is the winter of our[2] discontent
    Made glorious[3] summer by this son[4] of York,[5]
    And all the clouds that loured[6] upon our house[7]
    In[8] the deep bosom of the ocean buried.[9]

1 Duke of Gloucester, whose given name is Richard
2 although high nobility, especially members of royal families, often spoke of
  themselves in the first person plural ("we"), rather than the first person
  singular ("I"),★ Richard here speaks here of his family, not himself
3 brilliant, splendid
4 son (King Edward IV, Richard's brother, whose often tumultuous reign
  nevertheless lasted twenty-one years) (with a pun on "sun," Edward's chosen
  emblem)
5 the royal house/family★
6 frowned, scowled★
7 lineage, family★
8 are in
9 IN the deep BUzum OF the Oshun BEReed (the metrically reversed first
  foot, apparently signaling trochaic rather than iambic prosody, is historically a
  common poetic device; the rest of the line is unimpeachably iambic)

5   Now are our brows bound[10] with victorious wreaths,

Our bruisèd arms[11] hung up for monuments,[12]

Our stern alarums[13] changed to merry meetings,[14]

Our dreadful marches[15] to delightful measures.[16]

Grim-visaged war hath smoothed his wrinkled front,[17]

10   And now, instead of mounting barbèd[18] steeds

To fright the souls of fearful[19] adversaries,

He capers[20] nimbly in a lady's chamber[21]

To the lascivious pleasing of a lute.

But I, that am not shaped[22] for sportive tricks,[23]

15   Nor made to court an amorous looking-glass[24] –

I, that am rudely stamped,[25] and want[26] love's majesty[27]

To strut[28] before a wanton ambling[29] nymph –

I, that am curtailed[30] of this fair proportion,[31]

10 encircled
11 bruisèd arms = battered armor★
12 for monuments = as symbols of commemoration
13 stern alarums = austere/grim calls to arms/battle★
14 gatherings
15 dreadful marches = dangerous/formidable troop movements
16 music, dancing
17 forehead
18 wearing protective or decorative breast armor
19 frightened, anxious★
20 dances
21 parlor
22 created, fashioned, formed
23 sportive tricks = playful/frolicking pranks/feats
24 court an amorous looking-glass = pay careful attention to a fond/loving mirror
25 rudely stamped = ruggedly/harshly created/made
26 lack★
27 power
28 swagger, show off
29 wanton ambling = unrestrained/frolicsome/lewd walking
30 docked (as a dog's tail is docked – i.e., cut off)
31 fair proportion = pleasing/delightful/desirable★ capability, share★

Cheated of feature[32] by dissembling[33] nature,
Deformed, unfinished, sent before my time   20
Into this breathing[34] world, scarce half made up[35]
(And that so lamely and unfashionable
That dogs bark at me as I halt[36] by them),
Why I, in this weak piping time[37] of peace,
Have no delight[38] to pass away the time,   25
Unless to see my shadow in the sun
And descant on[39] mine own deformity.
And therefore, since I cannot prove[40] a lover,
To entertain[41] these fair well-spoken days
I am determined[42] to prove a villain[43]   30
And hate the idle[44] pleasures of these days.
Plots have I laid, inductions[45] dangerous,
By[46] drunken prophecies,[47] libels, and dreams,
To set my brother Clarence[48] and the King
In deadly hate the one against the other.   35

32 (1) comeliness, (2) good proportions
33 deceiving, hypocritical
34 living (as a newborn baby enters on life by breathing)
35 made up = completed
36 limp★
37 weak piping = peaceful/pastoral (rather than martial) flute-playing rhythm
38 (noun) joy, pleasure
39 descant on = describe, hold forth (sing about)
40 establish myself as
41 (1) maintain, sustain, (2) deal with, admit★
42 am determined = have chosen/decided★
43 scoundrel★
44 empty, useless★
45 beginnings, introductions★
46 by means of
47 prophetic utterances
48 Duke of Clarence; his given name is George (he is older than Richard, younger than Edward)

And if King Edward be as true[49] and just
As I am subtle,[50] false,[51] and treacherous,
This day should Clarence closely be mewed[52] up,
About[53] a prophecy which says that "G"
40   Of Edward's heirs[54] the murderer shall be.
Dive,[55] thoughts, down to my soul, here
Clarence comes.

ENTER CLARENCE, GUARDED, AND SIR ROBERT BRAKENBURY,
CONSTABLE[56] OF THE TOWER OF LONDON

Brother, good day. What means this armèd guard
That waits upon[57] your Grace?

Clarence   His Majesty,
45   Tend'ring[58] my person's[59] safety, hath appointed[60]
This conduct to convey[61] me to the Tower.

Gloucester Upon what cause?

Clarence   Because my name is George.

Gloucester Alack, my lord, that fault is none of yours.
He should, for that, commit[62] your godfathers.
50   O belike[63] his Majesty hath some intent

49 steadfast, trusty★
50 artful, skillful, cunning, sly★
51 deceitful, lying★
52 closely be mewed = secretly★ be cooped/caged★
53 in reference to, in connection with
54 i.e., his two young sons, Edward and Richard
55 disappear, hide
56 chief officer
57 waits upon = watches over
58 feeling tender/solicitous for
59 living body★
60 arranged
61 conduct [noun] to convey = escort★ to lead/bring★
62 put in/send to prison
63 perhaps★

That you shall be new-christened in the Tower.
But what's the matter, Clarence, may I know?
Clarence   Yea, Richard, when I know, for I protest[64]
As yet I do not. But as[65] I can learn,
He hearkens after[66] prophecies and dreams,   55
And from the cross-row[67] plucks the letter "G,"
And says a wizard told him that by "G"
His issue[68] disinherited should be.
And for[69] my name of George begins with "G,"
It follows in his thought that I am he.   60
These (as I learn) and such like toys[70] as these
Have moved[71] his Highness to commit me now.
Gloucester Why this it is, when men are ruled[72] by women.
'Tis not the king that sends you to the Tower,
My Lady Grey[73] his wife, Clarence, 'tis she   65
That tempts[74] him to this extremity.
Was it not she and that good man of worship,[75]
Anthony Woodville,[76] her brother there,

64 declare★
65 as far as
66 hearkens after = pays attention/listens to
67 alphabet
68 children★
69 because, since
70 tricks, amusements★
71 stirred★
72 controlled, guided
73 Elizabeth Woodville (1437–1492), daughter of the first Earl Rivers (d. 1469),
   married Edward IV (1464), having originally married Sir John Grey (1432–
   1461), who was killed in the second battle of Albans; reference to the
   reigning queen by her former title is intentionally rude
74 pushes
75 honor, repute, standing: "good man" being a form of address used for people
   of lower, non-gentlemanly rank, this remark too is intentionally rude
76 2nd Earl Rivers

That made him send Lord Hastings to the Tower,
70 From whence this present day he is delivered?[77]
We are not safe Clarence, we are not safe.

Clarence   By heaven, I think there is no man secure
But the Queen's kindred and night-walking heralds[78]
That trudge betwixt the King and Mistress[79] Shore.[80]
75 Heard ye not what an humble suppliant
Lord Hastings was to her[81] for his delivery?

Gloucester   Humbly complaining to her deity[82]
Got my Lord Chamberlain[83] his liberty.
I'll tell you what, I think it is our way,[84]
80 If we will keep[85] in favor with the King,
To be her men and wear her livery.[86]
The jealous o'erworn[87] widow[88] and herself,
Since that our brother dubbed[89] them gentlewomen,[90]
Are mighty gossips[91] in our monarchy.[92]

---

77 freed★
78 messengers/go-betweens, rather than true heralds
79 Mrs.★ (but see note 80, just below)
80 Edward IV's mistress, Jane Shore, wife of a London commoner (in fact, by
then she was no longer Edward's mistress but had become the mistress of
Lord Hastings)
81 Queen Elizabeth
82 godhead
83 Hastings
84 path, road★
85 will keep = wish to stay/hold/preserve ourselves
86 servants' uniforms
87 jealous o'erworn = vigilant/solicitous/zealous★ threadbare, obsolete
88 Queen Margaret, Henry VI's widow
89 dub = to confer a rank upon someone
90 women of noble/high birth
91 spreaders of rumor
92 kingdom★

Brakenbury I beseech your Graces both to pardon me.   85
  His Majesty hath straitly given in charge[93]
  That no man shall have private conference[94]
  (Of what degree[95] soever) with your brother.

Gloucester Even so,[96] and please your worship, Brakenbury,
  You may partake of[97] any thing we say: 90
  We speak no treason, man. We say the King
  Is wise and virtuous, and his noble queen
  Well struck in[98] years, fair, and not jealous.
  We say that Shore's wife hath a pretty[99] foot,
  A cherry lip, a bonny[100] eye, a passing[101] pleasing tongue,   95
  And that the Queen's kindred are[102] made gentlefolks.[103]
  How say you sir? Can you deny all this?

Brakenbury With this (my lord) myself have nought to do.

Gloucester Naught[104] to do with Mistress Shore? I tell thee,
  fellow,
  He that doth naught with her (excepting one)   100
  Were best to do it secretly, alone.

Brakenbury What one, my lord?

93 straitly given in charge = strictly/urgently★ commanded★
94 conversation★
95 no man of what rank★
96 quite/just/exactly★ so
97 partake of = share in
98 struck in = marked by
99 excellent/pleasing/dainty (men's legs were freely displayed, women's were
  hidden by long skirts, but feet could not so easily be hidden)
100 pleasing
101 surpassing, extremely
102 have been
103 people of noble/high birth★
104 wickedness, immorality

Gloucester   Her husband, knave.[105] Wouldst thou betray me?

Brakenbury   I do beseech your Grace

105   To pardon me, and withal forbear[106]

Your conference with the noble Duke.

Clarence   We know thy charge, Brakenbury, and will obey.

Gloucester   We are the Queen's abjects,[107] and must obey.

Brother farewell, I will[108] unto the King,

110   And whatsoever you will employ[109] me in,

Were[110] it to call King Edward's widow[111] sister,[112]

I will perform[113] it to enfranchise[114] you.

Meantime, this deep disgrace in[115] brotherhood

Touches[116] me deeper than you can imagine.

115 *Clarence*   I know it pleaseth neither of us well.

Gloucester   Well, your imprisonment shall not be long,

I will deliver you or else lie[117] for you.

Meantime, have patience.

Clarence   I must perforce.[118] Farewell.

EXEUNT[119] CLARENCE, BRAKENBURY, AND GUARD

105 rascal
106 withal forbear = also/at the same time/moreover★ give up★
107 downcast subjects
108 will go
109 use, make use of★
110 even if it were
111 i.e., the widow he married, the queen
112 in-law designations were not used: a brother's wife was (or should be) your
     sister, not your sister-in-law
113 do, complete★
114 liberate, set free
115 of
116 strikes, hits, affects★
117 (1) exchange places, (2) tell lies
118 of necessity, by constraint of physical force★
119 Latin plural of "exit"★

Gloucester Go tread[120] the path that thou shalt ne'er return.

Simple, plain[121] Clarence, I do love thee so   120

That I will shortly send thy soul to heaven,

If heaven will take the present at our[122] hands.

But who comes here? The new-delivered Hastings?

ENTER HASTINGS

Hastings Good time of day unto my gracious[123] lord.

Gloucester As much unto my good Lord Chamberlain. 125

Well are you[124] welcome to the open air.

How hath your lordship brooked[125] imprisonment?

Hastings With patience (noble lord) as prisoners must.

But I shall live (my lord) to give them thanks

That were the cause of my imprisonment.   130

Gloucester No doubt, no doubt, and so shall Clarence too,

For they that were your enemies are his,

And have prevailed[126] as much on him as you.

Hastings More pity[127] that the eagles should be mewed

While kites and buzzards prey[128] at liberty.[129]   135

Gloucester What news abroad?[130]

Hastings No news so bad abroad as this at home.

The King is sickly, weak, and melancholy,

---

120 walk
121 uncomplicated, weak, silly★
122 my
123 pleasant, charming, courteous (formal usage)★
124 well are you = you are very
125 endured, put up with★
126 been successful/superior/stronger★
127 more pity = more's the pity, what a shame
128 kites and buzzards prey = falcons and low-grade hawks who steal/rob★
129 at liberty = without hindrance, freely
130 current, at large in the world (i.e., away from where we are)★

And his physicians fear[131] him mightily.

140 *Gloucester* Now, by Saint John, this news is bad indeed.

O he hath kept an evil diet[132] long,

And overmuch consumed[133] his royal person.

'Tis very grievous to be thought upon.

What, is he in his bed?

145 *Hastings*   He is.

Gloucester Go you before,[134] and I will follow you.

EXIT HASTINGS

He cannot live, I hope, and must not die

Till George be packed with post-horse[135] up to heaven.

I'll in, to urge his hatred more to Clarence,

150 With lies well steeled[136] with weighty arguments,

And if I fail not in my deep intent

Clarence hath not another day to live.

Which done, God take King Edward to his mercy,

And leave the world for me to bustle[137] in,

155 For then I'll marry Warwick's[138] youngest daughter.[139]

What though I killed her husband and her father?

---

131 fear for

132 way of life

133 used up, wasted

134 as Lord Chamberlain – the court official directly responsible for the King's
living quarters – Hastings had more ready access to the King than anyone,
even the King's brother

135 packed with post-horse = transported by fast, ★ hired horses

136 backed (coated with steel, like the back of a mirror)

137 be energetically active

138 Richard Beauchamp, Earl of Warwick (1428–1471), known as "the
kingmaker"

139 Lady Anne Neville

The readiest way to make the wench[140] amends
Is to become her husband and her father.[141]
The which will I, not all[142] so much for love
As for another secret close[143] intent,   160
By marrying her, which[144] I must reach unto.[145]
But yet I run before my horse to market.
Clarence still breathes, Edward still lives and reigns:
When they are gone, then must I count my gains.

EXIT

---

140 young woman (in familiar usage)
141 i.e., by replacing her prior father-in-law, Henry VI, by the process of
     replacing him as king
142 entirely
143 concealed, hidden
144 who
145 reach unto = obtain

SCENE 2

London, Another street

ENTER CORSE[1] OF KING HENRY VI WITH ARMED GUARDS,
LADY ANNE BEING THE MOURNER

Anne Set down, set down your honorable load,
If honor may be shrouded[2] in a hearse,
Whilst I awhile obsequiously[3] lament
Th' untimely[4] fall of virtuous Lancaster.[5]
5   Poor key-cold figure[6] of a holy king,
Pale ashes[7] of the house of Lancaster,
Thou bloodless remnant of that royal blood!
Be it lawful[8] that I invocate[9] thy ghost,
To hear the lamentations of poor Anne,
10   Wife to thy Edward, to thy slaughtered son,[10]
Stabbed by the selfsame hand[11] that made these wounds!
Lo, in these windows that let forth[12] thy life,
I pour the helpless balm of my poor eyes.[13]

---

1 corpse★
2 concealed, enveloped
3 dutifully
4 premature★
5 Henry VI
6 key-cold figure = body as cold as a metal key ("dead")
7 remains
8 theologically permissible (i.e., Henry VI was not a saint, to whom prayers could be properly addressed)
9 pray to, invoke
10 killed in battle, in 1471, by troops associated with Richard, though not by him personally
11 again, Richard may have been linked to Henry VI's death, but there is no evidence that he was the assassin; Edward IV, Richard's brother, is far more likely to have been behind the murder
12 that let forth = wounds through which your life (spirit) came out★
13 i.e., her tears

O cursed be the hand that made these holes![14]
Cursed the heart, that had the heart to do it!   15
Cursed the blood,[15] that let[16] this blood from hence!
More direful hap betide[17] that hated wretch
That makes us wretched by the death of thee,
Than[18] I can wish to adders, spiders, toads,
Or any creeping venomed thing that lives!   20
If ever he have child, abortive[19] be it,
Prodigious,[20] and untimely brought to light,
Whose ugly and unnatural aspect[21]
May fright the hopeful[22] mother at the view,
And that[23] be heir to his unhappiness![24]   25
If ever he have wife, let her be made
More miserable[25] by the death of him
As I am made by my poor lord[26] and thee!
(*to corpse-bearers*) Come now toward Chertsey[27] with your
holy load,
Taken from Paul's[28] to be interrèd there.   30
And still as you are[29] weary of the weight,

14 0 CURSED be the HAND that MADE these HOLES (*or* 0 CURsed BE …)
15 life
16 discharged, emitted
17 direful hap betide = terrible/awful★ fortune/luck★ befall/happen to★
18 than the fortune/luck
19 premature★
20 monstrous
21 appearance★
22 expectant
23 that child
24 his unhappiness = Richard's (1) fortune, luck, (2) wrongdoing, evil
25 MIzaRAble
26 husband
27 abbey on the Thames River★
28 St. Paul's Cathedral, London★
29 still as you are = since you are still

Rest you, whiles I lament King Henry's corse.

Gloucester   Stay[30] you that bear the corse, and set it down.

Anne   What black[31] magician conjures up this fiend,

35   To stop devoted charitable[32] deeds?

Gloucester   Villains,[33] set down the corse or by Saint Paul

I'll make a corse of him that disobeys.

Gentleman   My lord, stand back and let the coffin pass.

Gloucester   Unmannered[34] dog, stand'st[35] thou, when I

command!

40   Advance[36] thy halbert[37] higher than my breast,

Or by Saint Paul I'll strike thee to my foot

And spurn[38] upon thee, beggar, for thy boldness.

Anne   What, do you tremble? Are you all afraid?

Alas, I blame you not, for you are mortal,

45   And mortal eyes cannot endure the devil.

Avaunt,[39] thou dreadful minister[40] of hell!

Thou hadst but[41] power over his[42] mortal body,

His soul thou canst not have. Therefore be gone.

30 stop★
31 foul, malignant, evil★
32 devoted charitable = consecrated benevolent/kindly (CHAriTAble)
33 low-born scoundrels
34 rude, unmannerly
35 stop, halt
36 lift★
37 spearlike weapon
38 trample, kick★
39 depart, go away
40 agent, servant★
41 just
42 the corpse, Henry VI

Gloucester   Sweet saint,[43] for charity,[44] be not so curst.[45]

Anne   Foul devil, for God's sake hence, and trouble us not,   50
  For thou hast made the happy[46] earth thy hell,
  Filled it with cursing cries, and deep exclaims.[47]
  If thou delight to view thy heinous deeds,
  Behold this pattern[48] of thy butcheries.
  O gentlemen, see, see, dead Henry's wounds   55
  Open their congealed[49] mouths and bleed afresh![50]
  Blush, blush, thou lump of foul deformity,
  For 'tis thy presence that exhales[51] this blood
  From cold and empty veins, where no blood dwells.
  Thy deeds, inhuman and unnatural,   60
  Provokes[52] this deluge most unnatural.
  O God, which this blood mad'st,[53] revenge his death!
  O earth, which this blood drink'st, revenge his death!
  Either heaven with lightning strike the murderer dead,
  Or earth gape open wide and eat him quick,[54]   65
  As thou dost swallow up this good king's blood

43 angel, person deserving of reverence
44 Christian love (*caritas*)★
45 hateful, virulent
46 lucky, fortunate★
47 outcries★
48 image, model (i.e., the corpse of Henry VI)
49 clotted, coagulated (Open their CONgealed MOUTHS and BLEED aFRESH)
50 (as dead bodies were supposed to do, when their murderer approached them)
51 draws forth★
52 calls forth, arouses, incites★ (subject-verb agreement was not always observed in Elizabethan English)
53 (i.e., all human beings are made/created by God)
54 alive★

Which his hell-governed[55] arm hath butcherèd!

Gloucester Lady, you know no rules[56] of charity,

Which[57] renders[58] good for bad, blessings for curses.

70 *Anne*   Villain, thou know'st no law of God nor man.

No beast so fierce but knows some touch[59] of pity.

Gloucester But I know none, and therefore am no beast.

Anne   O wonderful,[60] when devils tell the truth!

Gloucester More wonderful, when angels are so angry.

75 Vouchsafe[61] (divine perfection of a woman)

Of these supposèd crimes to give me leave,[62]

By circumstance,[63] but[64] to acquit myself.

Anne   Vouchsafe, diffused infection[65] of a man,

Of these known evils but to give me leave,

80 By circumstance, to curse thy cursèd self.

Gloucester Fairer than tongue can name[66] thee, let me have

Some patient[67] leisure to excuse myself.

Anne   Fouler than heart can think thee, thou canst make

No excuse current[68] but to hang thyself.

85 *Gloucester* By[69] such despair, I should[70] accuse myself.

55 hell-controlled/directed
56 principles, customs, habits
57 i.e., charity
58 returns, gives back
59 small quantity★
60 marvelous, astonishing★
61 grant, permit, agree★
62 permission
63 context, details
64 only
65 diffused infection = disordered/confused ("shapeless") corruption
66 describe
67 forbearing, lenient★
68 genuine★
69 by means of
70 would

Anne   And by despairing shouldst thou stand excused,

For doing worthy[71] vengeance on thyself,

Which didst unworthy slaughter upon others.

Gloucester Say[72] that I slew them not?

Anne   Then say they were not slain.   90

But dead they are, and – devilish slave[73] – by thee.

Gloucester I did not kill your husband.

Anne   Why, then he is alive.

Gloucester Nay, he is dead, and slain by Edward's hands.

Anne   In thy foul throat[74] thou liest! Queen Margaret saw   95

Thy murderous falchion[75] smoking in his blood,

The which thou once didst bend[76] against her breast,

But that[77] thy brothers beat[78] aside the point.

Gloucester I was provokèd by her sland'rous tongue,

Which laid their guilt upon my guiltless shoulders.   100

Anne   Thou wast provokèd by thy bloody mind,

Which never dreamt on aught[79] but butcheries.

Didst thou not kill this king?

Gloucester   I grant ye.[80]

Anne   Dost grant me, hedgehog? Then God grant me too

Thou mayst be damnèd for that wicked deed!   105

O he was gentle, mild, and virtuous!

Gloucester The better for the King of Heaven, that hath him.

71 excellent, good, honorable★
72 suppose
73 used as a term of contempt ("low person/servant")★
74 in thy foul throat = infamously
75 sword (FOILshun)
76 aim, direct, point★
77 but that = except
78 struck
79 anything
80 I grant ye = I agree/consent ("yes")

Anne   He is in heaven, where thou shalt never come.

Gloucester Let him thank me, that holp[81] to send him thither,

110   For he was fitter for that place than earth.[82]

Anne   And thou unfit for any place but hell.

Gloucester Yes, one place else, if you will hear me name it.

Anne   Some dungeon.

Gloucester   Your bedchamber.

Anne   Ill rest betide[83] the chamber where thou liest!

115 *Gloucester* So will it madam, till I lie with you.

Anne   I hope so!

Gloucester I know so. But gentle Lady Anne,

To leave this keen[84] encounter of our wits,[85]

And fall somewhat into a slower method.

120   Is not the causer of the timeless[86] deaths

Of these Plantagenets,[87] Henry and Edward,

As blameful as the executioner?

Anne   Thou wast the cause, and most accursed effect.[88]

Gloucester Your beauty was the cause of that effect –

125   Your beauty, that did haunt[89] me in my sleep

To undertake[90] the death of all the world,

So I might live one hour in your sweet bosom.

Anne   If I thought that, I tell thee, homicide,[91]

---

81 helped
82 (Henry VI had been more or less feebleminded for many years)
83 ill rest betide = bad rest/sleeping occur/befall
84 clever, sharp
85 minds, intelligence★
86 premature, unseasonable, untimely
87 a royal lineage (planTAdgenETS)
88 operative influence
89 regularly come to me
90 pledge/commit myself to
91 murderer★

These nails should rend[92] that beauty from my cheeks.

Gloucester These eyes could never endure that beauty's 　　　　130
wrack[93] –

You should not blemish[94] it, if I stood by.[95]

As all the world is cheerèd by the sun,

So I by that. It is my day, my life.

Anne Black night o'ershade[96] thy day, and death thy life!

Gloucester Curse not thyself, fair creature, thou art both.　　135

Anne I would[97] I were, to be revenged on thee.

Gloucester It is a quarrel most unnatural,

To be revenged on him that loveth you.

Anne It is a quarrel just and reasonable,[98]

To be revenged on him that killed my husband.　　　　140

Gloucester He that bereft thee, lady, of thy husband,

Did it to help thee to a better husband.

Anne His better doth not breathe upon the earth.

Gloucester He lives that loves thee better than he could.

Anne Name him.

Gloucester 　　　　　　Plantagenet.

Anne 　　　　　　　　　　Why, that was he.　　145

Gloucester The selfsame name, but one of better nature.[99]

Anne Where is he?

Gloucester 　　　　　　Here. (*she spits at him*) Why dost thou
spit at me?

92 tear
93 destruction
94 damage, spoil, ruin★
95 nearby★
96 darken
97 wish★
98 REEZaNAHble
99 character

Anne   Would it were mortal poison, for thy sake!

Gloucester Never came poison from so sweet a place.

150 Anne   Never hung poison on a fouler toad.

            Out of my sight! Thou dost infect my eyes.

Gloucester Thine eyes (sweet lady) have infected mine.

Anne   Would they were basilisks,[100] to strike thee dead!

Gloucester I would they were, that I might die at once,

155   For now they kill me with a living death.

            Those eyes of thine from mine have drawn salt tears,

            Shamed their aspects with store[101] of childish drops.

            These eyes, which never shed remorseful tear,

            No, when my father York and Edward wept,

160   To hear the piteous moan that Rutland[102] made

            When black-faced Clifford[103] shook his sword at him,

            Nor when thy warlike father, like a child,

            Told the sad story of my father's death,

            And twenty times made pause to sob and weep,

165   That all the standers-by had wet their cheeks

            Like trees bedashed with[104] rain. In that sad time

            My manly eyes did scorn an humble[105] tear.

            And what these sorrows could not thence exhale

            Thy beauty hath, and made them blind with weeping.

170   I never sued[106] to friend nor enemy.

---

100 mythological reptile, whose very look could kill (BAsiLISKS)★
101 an abundance
102 his brother Edmund, Earl of Rutland, murdered at age 17 (see *3 Henry VI*, 1.3)
103 John de Clifford (1435–1461), nicknamed "the Butcher" for his cruelty
104 bedashed with = beaten/smashed★ by
105 low, commonplace
106 (1) appealed, petitioned, (2) wooed, courted

My tongue could never learn sweet smoothing[107] word.
But now[108] thy beauty is proposed my fee,[109]
My proud heart sues, and prompts[110] my tongue to speak.

SHE LOOKS SCORNFULLY AT HIM

Teach not thy lip such scorn, for it was made
For kissing, lady, not for such contempt.   175
If thy revengeful heart cannot forgive,
Lo, here I lend[111] thee this sharp-pointed sword,
Which if thou please to hide[112] in this true[113] breast,
And let the soul[114] forth[115] that adoreth thee,
I lay it naked[116] to the deadly stroke,   180
And humbly beg the death upon my knee.

HE KNEELS AND UNCOVERS HIS BREAST;
SHE AIMS THE SWORD AT IT

Nay, do not pause, for I did kill King Henry,
But 'twas thy beauty that provoked me.
Nay, now dispatch.[117] 'Twas I that stabbed young Edward,
But 'twas thy heavenly face that set[118] me on.   185

SHE LETS THE SWORD FALL

107 flattering, pleasant, calm★
108 now that
109 proposed my fee = presented as my remuneration/reward
110 incites, moves, urges
111 give
112 bury
113 constant, faithful
114 SOel
115 come out
116 bare★
117 (1) kill, get rid/dispose of, ★ (2) do it quickly
118 urged

Take up the sword again, or take up me.[119]

Anne   Arise, dissembler.[120] Though I wish thy death,
        I will not be thy executioner.

Gloucester (rising) Then bid me kill myself, and I will do it.

Anne   I have already.

190 Gloucester   That was in thy rage.
        Speak it again, and even with[121] the word
        That hand, which for thy love, did kill thy love,
        Shall, for thy love, kill a far truer love.
        To both their deaths shalt thou be accessary.[122]

195 Anne   I would I knew thy heart.

Gloucester 'Tis figured[123] in my tongue.

Anne   I fear me both are false.

Gloucester Then never man was true.

Anne   Well, well, put up[124] your sword.

200 Gloucester Say, then, my peace is made.

Anne   That shall you know hereafter.

Gloucester But shall I live in hope?

Anne   All men I hope live so.

Gloucester Vouchsafe to wear this ring.

205 Anne   To take is not to give.

Gloucester (puts ring on her finger) Look, how my ring
        encompasseth[125] thy finger.

---

119 take up me = (1) raise from his kneeling position, (2) accept, receive,
    embrace, espouse
120 deceiver, hypocrite★
121 even with = exactly at
122 contributor, participant
123 portrayed, represented
124 away, sheathe
125 surrounds, encloses

24

Even so thy breast encloseth my poor heart.
Wear both of them, for both of them are thine.
And if thy poor devoted servant may
But beg one favor at thy gracious hand,   210
Thou dost confirm his happiness for ever.

Anne   What is it?

Gloucester That it would please thee leave these sad designs[126]
To him that hath more cause to be a mourner,
And presently repair[127] to Crosby House,   215
Where – after I have solemnly interred[128]
At Chertsey monast'ry this noble king,
And wet his grave with my repentant tears –
I will with all expedient duty[129] see you.
For divers unknown[130] reasons, I beseech you   220
Grant me this boon.[131]

Anne   With all my heart, and much it joys me too,
To see you are become so penitent.
Tressel and Berkeley,[132] go along with me.

Gloucester Bid me farewell.

Anne   'Tis more than you deserve.   225
But since you teach me how to flatter you,
Imagine I have said farewell already.

EXEUNT LADY ANNE, TRESSEL, AND BERKELEY

126 projects, purposes★
127 presently repair = at once★ go★
128 where AFter I have SOlemnLY inTERRED
129 expedient duty = (1) proper/suitable (2) speedy respect/deference
130 divers unknown = various undisclosed/secret
131 request, petition, favor★
132 BARKlee

Gentlemen Toward Chertsey, noble lord?
Gloucester No. To Whitefriars,[133] there attend[134] my coming.

EXEUNT ALL BUT GLOUCESTER

230   Was ever woman in this humor[135] wooed?
      Was ever woman in this humor won?
      I'll have her, but I will not keep her long.
      What? I that killed her husband, and his father,
      To take her in her heart's extremest hate,
235   With curses in her mouth, tears in her eyes,
      The bleeding witness of her[136] hatred by,
      Having God, her conscience, and these bars[137] against me,
      And I, no friends to back my suit[138] withal,
      But the plain devil,[139] and dissembling looks?
240   And yet to win her? All the world to[140] nothing!
      Ha!
      Hath she forgot already that brave prince,
      Edward, her lord, whom I, some three months since,
      Stabbed in my angry mood at Tewkesbury?[141]
245   A sweeter[142] and a lovelier gentleman,
      Framed[143] in the prodigality[144] of nature,

133 monastery in central London
134 wait for/upon★
135 style, mood, state★
136 the Folio: "my"
137 (noun) barriers, obstructions
138 pursuit, supplication★
139 plain devil = complete roguery/knavery/energetic recklessness
140 against, compared to
141 battle in which Yorkists defeated Lancastrians
142 more agreeable/delightful/pleasant
143 formed, fashioned★
144 lavishness, abundance

Young, valiant, wise, and (no doubt) right[145] royal,

The spacious world cannot again afford.[146]

And will she yet abase[147] her eyes on me,

That cropped[148] the golden prime of this sweet prince, 250

And made her widow to a woeful bed?

On me, whose all not equals Edward's moiety?[149]

On me, that halts, and am unshapen[150] thus?

My dukedom to a beggarly denier,[151]

I do[152] mistake my person all this while. 255

Upon my life, she finds (although I cannot)

Myself to be a marv'lous proper[153] man.

I'll be at charges for[154] a looking-glass,

And entertain a score[155] or two of tailors,

To study fashions to adorn my body. 260

Since I am crept in[156] favor with myself,

I will maintain it with some little cost.

But first I'll turn[157] yon fellow[158] in his grave,

And then return lamenting to my love.

145 completely, truly★

146 manage, provide, produce★

147 humiliate, lower

148 cut off

149 share, portion★ (MOYehTEE)

150 deformed

151 to a beggarly denier = wagered against a miserable little coin

152 (used as an intensifier: "do mistake" = very much mistake)

153 marvelous proper = astonishingly distinctive / perfect / handsome

154 at charges for = at the expense of

155 twenty

156 crept in = stolen into

157 deposit

158 Henry VI

265 Shine out, fair sun, till I have bought a glass,[159]
That[160] I may see my shadow as I pass.

EXIT

159 mirror
160 so that

SCENE 3

The palace

ENTER QUEEN ELIZABETH, RIVERS, AND GREY

Rivers   Have patience madam, there's no doubt his Majesty[1]

Will soon recover his accustomed health.

Grey   (*to Elizabeth*) In that[2] you brook it ill, it makes him

worse.

Therefore for God's sake entertain good comfort,

And cheer his Grace with quick[3] and merry words.   5

Elizabeth If he were dead, what would betide on me?

Rivers   No other harm but loss of such a lord.[4]

Elizabeth The loss of such a lord includes all harm.

Grey   The heavens have blessed you with a goodly[5] son,

To be your comforter when he is gone.   10

Elizabeth Oh, he is young and his minority

Is put unto the trust of Richard Gloucester,

A man that loves not me, nor none of you.

Rivers   Is it concluded he shall be Protector?[6]

Elizabeth It is determined, not concluded[7] yet.   15

But so it must be, if the King miscarry.[8]

ENTER BUCKINGHAM AND STANLEY[9]

1 Edward IV
2 in that = because, since
3 lively★
4 husband
5 handsome, fair★
6 guardian, regent★
7 finalized
8 die★
9 Derby

Grey	Here come the lords of Buckingham and Derby.[10]
Buckingham	*(to the Queen)* Good time of day unto your royal Grace!
Stanley	God make your Majesty joyful[11] as you have been!
Elizabeth	The Countess Richmond,[12] good my Lord of Derby,

To your good prayers will scarcely say amen.
Yet Derby, notwithstanding she's your wife,
And loves not me, be you good lord assured
I hate not you for her proud arrogance.

Stanley	I do beseech you, either not believe

The envious slanders of her false accusers,
Or if she be accused on true report,
Bear with her weakness, which I think proceeds
From wayward sickness,[13] and no grounded[14] malice.

Rivers	Saw you the King today, my Lord of Derby?
Stanley	But[15] now the Duke of Buckingham and I

Are come from visiting his Majesty.

Elizabeth	What likelihood of his amendment,[16] lords?
Buckingham	Madam good hope, his Grace speaks cheerfully.
Elizabeth	God grant him health, did you confer with him?
Buckingham	Aye, madam, he desires to make atonement[17]

Between the Duke of Gloucester and your brothers,[18]

10 Lord Stanley
11 as joyful
12 Derby's wife
13 wayward sickness = perverse/self-willed/wrongheaded★ ill health
14 firmly founded
15 just
16 recovery
17 harmony, concord
18 Rivers is one of her brothers

And betwixt them and my[19] Lord Chamberlain,[20]
And sent to warn[21] them to his royal presence.

Elizabeth   Would all were well. But that will never be.   40
I fear our happiness is at the height.

ENTER GLOUCESTER, HASTINGS, AND DORSET

Gloucester   They do me wrong, and I will not endure it.
Who is it that complains unto the King
That I (forsooth)[22] am stern,[23] and love them not?
By holy Paul, they love his Grace but lightly   45
That fill his ears with such dissentious[24] rumors.
Because I cannot flatter and speak fair,
Smile in men's faces, smooth, deceive, and cog,[25]
Duck[26] with French nods[27] and apish[28] courtesy,
I must be held a rancorous[29] enemy!   50
Cannot a plain man live, and think no harm,
But thus his simple truth must be abused
By silken,[30] sly, insinuating Jacks?[31]

Grey   To whom in all this presence[32] speaks your Grace?

19 the
20 Hastings
21 command
22 truly
23 uncompromising, austere, inflexible
24 quarrelsome, discordant
25 cheat
26 bow, stoop
27 quick head movements, by way of signaling
28 affected
29 grudging, spiteful★
30 elegant, flattering
31 knaves, common fellows★
32 company★

55 *Gloucester* To thee, that hast nor[33] honesty nor grace.[34]
 When have I injured thee? When done thee wrong?
 (*to Rivers*) Or thee? Or thee?[35] Or any of your faction?[36]
 A plague upon you all! His royal Grace
 (Whom God preserve better than you would wish)
60 Cannot be quiet[37] scarce a breathing while,
 But you must trouble him with lewd[38] complaints.
 Elizabeth Brother of Gloucester, you mistake the matter.
 The King, of his own royal disposition,[39]
 And not provoked by any suitor else,
65 Aiming (belike) at your interior[40] hatred,
 Which in your outward actions shows itself
 Against my children, brothers, and myself,
 Makes[41] him to send, that he may learn the ground.[42]
 Gloucester I cannot tell, the world is grown so bad
70 That wrens make prey where eagles dare not perch.
 Since every Jack became a gentleman
 There's many a gentle person made a Jack.
 Elizabeth Come, come, we know your meaning, brother
 Gloucester.
 You envy my advancement[43] and my friends.'

33 neither
34 (1) virtue, ★ (2) a duchess' title
35 Dorset?
36 party
37 peaceful, at rest★
38 vulgar, ignorant, ill-mannered
39 plan, arrangement, order
40 inner
41 causes
42 basis
43 preferment, achievement of higher rank, raising up★

God grant we never may have need of you!　　　　　　75

Gloucester　Meantime, God grants that I have need of you.

Our brother is imprisoned by your means,

Myself disgraced, and the nobility

Held in contempt, whilst great promotions[44]

Are daily given to ennoble those　　　　　　　　80

That scarce some two days since were worth a noble.[45]

Elizabeth　By Him that raised[46] me to this careful[47] height

From that contented hap[48] which I enjoyed,

I never did incense[49] his Majesty

Against the Duke of Clarence,[50] but have been　　85

An earnest advocate to plead for him.

My lord, you do me shameful injury,

Falsely to draw me in[51] these vile suspects.[52]

Gloucester　You may deny that you were not the cause

Of my Lord Hastings' late[53] imprisonment.　　　90

Rivers　　She may, my lord, for —

Gloucester　She may, Lord Rivers, why, who knows not so?

She may do more, sir, than denying that.

She may help you to many fair preferments,[54]

And then deny her aiding hand therein,　　　　　95

44 proMOseeOWNZ
45 (1) gold coin, (2) noble rank
46 lifted, elevated★
47 sorrowful, mournful ("full of cares")
48 fortune
49 excite, inflame★
50 a notoriously greedy, arrogant, unreliable man
51 into
52 suspicions
53 recent★
54 advancements, promotions★

And lay[55] those honors on your high deserts.[56]

What may she not? She may, aye, marry,[57] may she –

Rivers   What,[58] marry, may she?

Gloucester What, marry, may she? Marry with a king,

100   A bachelor, and a handsome stripling[59] too.

Iwis[60] your grandam[61] had a worser match.

Elizabeth My Lord of Gloucester, I have too long borne[62]

Your blunt upbraidings[63] and your bitter scoffs.[64]

By heaven, I will acquaint his Majesty

105   With those gross taunts[65] that oft I have endured.

I had rather[66] be a country servant maid

Than a great queen, with this condition,[67]

To be so baited,[68] scorned, and stormèd[69] at.

ENTER QUEEN MARGARET, UNSEEN
(AT THE BACK OF THE STAGE)

Small joy have I in being England's queen.

110 *Margaret*   (*aside*) And lessened be that small, God I beseech him!

55 attribute, bestow
56 high deserts = great merits★
57 indeed★
58 just what
59 young fellow (an indirect but insulting reference to her age)
60 Iwis = certainly, surely
61 grandmother★
62 endured★
63 blunt upbraidings = insensitive/rude/harsh/abrupt★ reproaches
64 mockery, ridicule
65 gross taunts = flagrant/monstrous sarcasms/gibes/insults
66 sooner, instead★
67 state, position, nature (kunDIseeOWN)★
68 baited = molested, harassed, tormented
69 raged

Thy honor, state,[70] and seat[71] is due to me.

Gloucester What? Threat you me with telling of the King?

Tell him, and spare not. Look, what I have said

I will avouch't[72] in presence of the King.

I dare adventure[73] to be sent to th'Tower.   115

'Tis time to speak, my pains[74] are quite[75] forgot.

Margaret (*aside*) Out, devil! I do remember them[76] too well.

Thou killed my husband Henry in the Tower,

And Edward, my poor son, at Tewkesbury.

Gloucester Ere you were queen, aye, or your husband king,   120

I was a pack-horse[77] in his great affairs,

A weeder-out of his proud adversaries,

A liberal[78] rewarder of his friends.

To royalize his blood, I spilt mine own.[79]

Margaret (*aside*) Yea, and much better blood than his, or thine.   125

Gloucester In all which time, you and your husband Grey

Were factious[80] for the house of Lancaster,

And Rivers, so were you. Was not your husband

In Margaret's battle[81] at Saint Alban's slain?

Let me put in your minds, if you forget,   130

What you have been ere now, and what you are.

70 (1) status, rank, (2) condition★
71 throne★
72 avouch't = state it and prove it
73 risk
74 efforts, labors, troubles
75 completely
76 his labors ("pains")
77 drudge
78 LIbeRAL
79 (i.e., in battle)
80 acting seditiously★
81 army★

Withal, what I have been, and what I am.

Margaret   (*aside*) A murderous villain, and so still thou art.

Gloucester Poor Clarence did forsake his father,[82] Warwick,

135   Yea, and forswore[83] himself – which Jesu pardon! –

Margaret   (*aside*) Which God revenge!

Gloucester To fight on[84] Edward's party,[85] for the crown,

And for his meed,[86] poor lord, he is mewed up.

I would to God my heart were flint, like Edward's,

140   Or Edward's soft and pitiful, like mine.

I am too childish-foolish for this world.

Margaret   (*aside*) Hie[87] thee to hell for shame, and leave
this world,

Thou cacodemon,[88] there thy kingdom is.

Rivers   My Lord of Gloucester, in those busy days

145   Which here you urge, to prove us enemies,

We followed then our lord, our lawful king.

So should we you, if you should be our king.

Gloucester If I should be? I had rather be a peddler.

Far be it from my heart, the thought thereof.

150 *Elizabeth* As little joy, my lord, as you suppose

You should enjoy, were you this country's king,

As little joy may you suppose in me,

That I enjoy, being the queen thereof.

Margaret   (*aside*) A little joy enjoys[89] the queen thereof,

82 father-in-law
83 i.e., repudiated ★ his pro-Warwick pledge and fought against Warwick
84 in
85 side★
86 reward★
87 hurry★
88 nightmare (KAkoDIEmen)
89 does indeed enjoy

For I am she, and altogether joyless.   155

I can no longer hold me patient.

MARGARET COMES FORWARD

Hear me, you wrangling pirates,[90] that fall out

In sharing that which you have pilled[91] from me!

Which of you trembles not that looks on me?

If not that I am queen, you bow like subjects,   160

Yet that, by you deposed, you quake like rebels?[92]

(*to Gloucester*) Ah gentle villain, do not turn away!

Gloucester   Foul wrinkled witch, what mak'st thou[93] in my sight?

Margaret   But[94] repetition of what thou hast marred,[95]

That will I make, before I let thee go.   165

Gloucester   Wert thou not banished, on pain[96] of death?

Margaret   I was. But I do find more pain in banishment

Than death can yield[97] me here by my abode.

A husband and a son thou owest to me,

(*to Elizabeth*) And thou a kingdom. All of you, allegiance.[98]   170

The sorrow that I have, by right is yours,

And all the pleasures you usurp are mine.

Gloucester   The curse my noble father laid on thee

When thou didst crown his warlike brows with paper[99]

90 wrangling pirates = quarrelsome★ robbers
91 plundered, robbed
92 If all of you bow like subjects, and not because I am *in fact* the Queen, then it
   must be that your guilt at having deposed me makes you tremble
93 mak'st thou = are you doing
94 only
95 destroyed, ruined
96 on pain = under penalty
97 give / give up, pay / pay for, allow★
98 owe me your duty
99 i.e., mocking his wish to be king by setting a paper crown on his head

175 And with thy scorns drew'st rivers from his eyes,
And then, to dry them, gav'st the Duke[100] a clout
Steeped[101] in the faultless[102] blood of pretty[103] Rutland –
His curses then, from bitterness of soul
Denounced[104] against thee, are all fall'n upon thee,
180 And God, not we, hath plagued thy bloody deed.

Elizabeth   So just is God, to right the innocent.

Hastings   O, 'twas the foulest deed to slay that babe,[105]
And the most merciless that e'er was heard of!

Rivers   Tyrants themselves wept when it was reported.

185 Dorset   No man but prophesied revenge for it.

Buckingham   Northumberland, then present, wept to see it.

Margaret   What? Were you snarling all before I came,
Ready to catch[106] each other by the throat,
And turn you all your hatred now on me?
190 Did York's dread curse prevail so much with heaven,
That Henry's death, my lovely Edward's death,
Their kingdom's loss, my woeful banishment,
Could all but answer[107] for that peevish[108] brat?
Can curses pierce the clouds and enter heaven?
195 Why then give way dull[109] clouds to my quick curses!
(to Elizabeth) Though not by war, by surfeit[110] die your king,

100 Richard's father was Duke of York
101 clout steeped = cloth/rag soaked
102 innocent
103 fine, pleasing, admirable
104 proclaimed, declared
105 Rutland (who was then 17)
106 seize
107 but answer = only be responsible/accountable
108 foolish★
109 senseless, stupid, sluggish★
110 excesses

As ours by[111] murder, to make him[112] a king!
Edward thy son, which now is Prince of Wales,
For Edward my son, which was Prince of Wales,
Die in his youth by like untimely violence!   200
Thyself a queen, for me that was a queen,
Outlive thy glory, like my wretched self!
Long mayst thou live to wail thy children's loss,
And see another, as I see thee now,
Decked[113] in thy rights, as thou art stalled[114] in mine!   205
Long die thy happy days before thy death,
And after many lengthened hours of grief
Die neither mother, wife, nor England's queen!
Rivers and Dorset, you were standers by,
And so wast thou, Lord Hastings, when my son   210
Was stabbed with bloody daggers. God I pray him
That none of you may live your natural age,
But by some unlooked accident[115] cut off!

Gloucester Have done thy charm,[116] thou hateful withered hag!

Margaret   And leave out thee? Stay dog, for thou shalt[117]   215
hear me.
If heaven have any grievous plague in store
Exceeding those that I can wish upon thee,
O let them keep it till thy sins be ripe,[118]
And then hurl down their indignation

111 did by
112 to make him = in order to make Edward IV
113 clothed, adorned
114 placed, put
115 unforeseen event
116 magical incantation★
117 must
118 ready, mature★

220   On thee, the troubler of the poor world's peace!
       The worm of conscience still[119] begnaw[120] thy soul!
       Thy friends suspect[121] for traitors while thou livest,
       And take deep[122] traitors for thy dearest friends!
       No sleep close up that deadly eye of thine,
225   Unless it be while some tormenting dream
       Affrights thee with a hell of ugly devils!
       Thou elvish-marked,[123] abortive, rooting[124] hog!
       Thou that wast sealed[125] in thy nativity[126]
       The slave of nature and the son of hell!
230   Thou slander[127] of thy mother's heavy womb!
       Thou loathèd issue[128] of thy father's loins,
       Thou rag[129] of honor, thou detested —

Gloucester Margaret.

Margaret   Richard.

Gloucester   Ha?

Margaret   I call thee not.

Gloucester I cry thee mercy[130] then, for I did think
235   That thou hadst called me all these bitter names.

Margaret Why so I did, but looked for no reply.

119 always, forever
120 corrode, chew at (biNAWE)
121 (verb)
122 great, profound, heinous
123 disfigured by peevish/evil supernatural creatures
124 grubbing
125 stamped
126 birth
127 defamation, insult, shame
128 child
129 tattered fragment
130 cry thee mercy = beg your pardon★

O let me make the period to[131] my curse!

Gloucester 'Tis done by me, and ends in "Margaret."

Elizabeth (*to Margaret*) Thus have you breathed your curse
   against yourself.

Margaret Poor painted[132] queen, vain flourish[133] of   240
   my fortune,[134]
   Why strew'st thou sugar on that bottled[135] spider,
   Whose deadly web ensnareth thee about?
   Fool, fool, thou whet'st[136] a knife to kill thyself.
   The day will come when thou shalt wish for me
   To help thee curse this poisonous bunchbacked[137] toad.   245

Hastings False-boding[138] woman, end thy frantic[139] curse,
   Lest to thy harm thou move our patience.

Margaret Foul shame upon you, you have all moved mine.

Rivers Were you well served,[140] you would be taught
   your duty.

Margaret To serve me well, you all should[141] do me duty,   250
   Teach me to be your queen, and you my subjects.
   O serve me well, and teach yourselves that duty!

Dorset Dispute not with her, she is lunatic.

---

131 make the period to = reach the end★ of
132 pretended, unreal
133 blossom, florid decoration★
134 good chance, luck★
135 swollen★ (his deformed back is a shape reminiscent of a bottle)
136 sharpen, prepare, ready★
137 humpbacked★
138 false-boding = wrongly predicting
139 lunatic★
140 well-served = properly attended to / waited upon (by underlings / servants)
141 would have to

Margaret   Peace, Master Marquess,[142] you are malapert,[143]

255   Your fire-new[144] stamp of honor is scarce current.[145]

O that your[146] young nobility could judge

What 'twere to lose it, and be[147] miserable![148]

They that stand high have many blasts to shake them,

And if they fall, they dash themselves to pieces.

260 Gloucester   Good counsel, marry. Learn it, learn it, Marquess.

Dorset   It touches you, my lord, as much as me.

Gloucester   Aye, and much more. But I was born so high

Our aerie buildeth[149] in the cedar's top,

And dallies[150] with the wind, and scorns the sun.

265 Margaret   And turns the sun to shade. Alas, alas,

Witness my son,[151] now in the shade of death,

Whose bright out-shining beams thy cloudy wrath

Hath in eternal darkness folded[152] up.

Your aerie buildeth in our aerie's nest.

270 O God that seest it, do not suffer[153] it.

As it is won with blood, lost be it so!

Buckingham   Peace, peace, for shame. If not, for[154] charity.

Margaret   Urge neither charity nor shame to me.

142 peace, Master Marquess = be silent, you boy with a count's title
143 saucy, impudent, presumptuous
144 fire-new = brand new
145 scare current = just barely effective
146 all the
147 thereafter to be
148 MIzaRAble
149 aerie buildeth = eagle's nest is built
150 amuses itself, sports, plays
151 witness my son = may my son bear witness★
152 shut
153 endure
154 then for

Uncharitably with me have you dealt,[155]
And shamefully my hopes (by you) are butchered. 275
My charity is outrage, life my shame,
And in that shame still live my sorrow's rage.

Buckingham Have done, have done.

Margaret   O princely Buckingham, I'll kiss thy hand
In sign of league and amity[156] with thee. 280
Now fair befall[157] thee, and thy noble house!
Thy garments are not spotted with our blood,
Nor thou within the compass[158] of my curse.

Buckingham Nor no one here, for curses never pass[159]
The lips of those that breathe them in the air. 285

Margaret   I will not think but they ascend the sky,
And there awake God's gentle-sleeping peace.
O Buckingham, take heed of yonder dog!
Look when he fawns, he bites, and when he bites
His venom tooth will rankle[160] to the death. 290
Have not to do with him, beware of him,
Sin, death, and hell have set their marks on him,
And all their ministers attend on him.

Gloucester   What doth she say, my Lord of Buckingham?

Buckingham Nothing that I respect,[161] my gracious lord. 295

Margaret   What, dost thou scorn me for my gentle counsel,
And soothe the devil that I warn thee from?

155 acted★
156 league and amity = alliance and friendship
157 come/happen to★
158 limits, measure
159 go any further than
160 fester, envenom
161 take into account, pay any attention to

O but remember this another day,

When he shall split thy very heart with sorrow,

300 And say[162] poor Margaret was a prophetess!

Live each of you the subjects to his hate,

And he to yours, and all of you to God's!

EXIT MARGARET

Hastings My hair doth stand on end to hear her curses.

Rivers And so doth mine, I muse[163] why she's at liberty.

305 *Gloucester* I cannot blame her, by God's holy Mother,

She hath had too much wrong, and I repent

My part thereof that I have done to her.

Elizabeth I never did her any, to my knowledge.

Gloucester Yet you have all the vantage[164] of her wrong.

310 I was too hot[165] to do somebody[166] good,

That[167] is too cold[168] in thinking of it now.

Marry, as for Clarence, he is well repaid,

He is franked up[169] to fatting for his pains,

God pardon them that are the cause thereof.

315 *Rivers* A virtuous and a Christian-like conclusion,

To pray for them that have done scathe[170] to us.

Gloucester So do I ever (*aside*), being well-advised,[171]

---

162 then say
163 ask myself, wonder
164 advantage, profit, gain
165 keen, zealous, eager
166 his older brother, Edward IV
167 who (Edward IV)
168 apathetic
169 franked up = penned it for feeding/cramming with food (i.e., readying animals for slaughter)★
170 harm, damage, hurt
171 prudent, wary, judicious★

For had I cursed now, I had cursed myself.

ENTER CATESBY

Catesby   Madam, his Majesty doth call for you,
   And for your Grace, and yours, my gracious lords.   320
Elizabeth   Catesby, I come. Lords, will you go with us?
Rivers   We wait upon your Grace.

EXEUNT ALL BUT GLOUCESTER

Gloucester I do the wrong, and first begin to brawl.[172]
   The secret mischiefs[173] that I set abroach[174]
   I lay unto the grievous[175] charge of others.   325
   Clarence, who I indeed have cast in darkness,
   I do beweep[176] to many simple gulls,[177]
   Namely, to Derby, Hastings, Buckingham,
   And tell them 'tis the Queen and her allies
   That stir[178] the King against the Duke my brother.   330
   Now they believe it, and withal whet me
   To be revenged on Rivers, Dorset, Grey.
   But then I sigh, and with a piece[179] of scripture
   Tell them that God bids us do good for evil.
   And thus I clothe my naked villainy   335
   With odd[180] old ends stol'n out of holy writ,[181]

172 squabble, scold, quarrel
173 evils
174 afloat, astir, afoot
175 oppressive
176 weep over
177 simple gulls = innocent fools / dupes
178 move*
179 bit, portion, fragment
180 assorted, diverse
181 with ODD old ENDS stol'n OUT of HOly WRIT

And seem a saint when most I play the devil.

ENTER TWO MURDERERS

But soft,[182] here come my executioners.[183]

How now, my hardy, stout, resolvèd mates,[184]

340   Are you now going to dispatch this thing?

Murderer 1   We are, my lord, and come to have the warrant[185]

That we may be admitted where he is.

Gloucester   Well thought upon, I have it here about[186] me.

(*gives the warrant*) When you have done, repair to

Crosby Place.

345   But sirs, be sudden[187] in the execution,[188]

Withal obdurate,[189] do not hear[190] him plead,

For Clarence is well-spoken, and perhaps

May move your hearts to pity if you mark[191] him.

Murderer 1   Tut, tut, my lord, we will not stand to prate,[192]

350   Talkers are no good doers, be assured.

We come to use our hands, and not our tongues.

Gloucester   Your eyes drop millstones, when fools' eyes

fall tears.[193]

---

182   quietly★

183   evil agents

184   hardy, stout, resolvèd mates = bold,★ brave, determined coworkers/
      colleagues/associates

185   (1) authorization, (2) guarantee★

186   on, with, in my pocket

187   speedy★

188   act, doing

189   hardened, stubborn, relentless (obDURet)★

190   listen to

191   pay attention to

192   chatter, talk★

193   your EYES drop MILLstones WHEN fools' EYES fall TEARS (N.B.: this is
      the prosody but not necessarily the pronunciation)

I like you, lads, about your business straight.[194]
Go, go, dispatch.

Murderer 1   We will, my noble lord.

EXEUNT

194 at once★

SCENE 4

London, The Tower

ENTER CLARENCE AND KEEPER[1]

Keeper   Why looks your Grace so heavily[2] today?
Clarence O, I have passed a miserable night,
　　So full of fearful dreams, of ugly sights,
　　That as I am a Christian faithful man
5　　I would not spend another such a night,
　　Though 'twere to buy a world of happy days,
　　So full of dismal terror was the time.
Keeper   What was your dream, my lord, I pray you tell me.
Clarence Methoughts[3] that I had broken[4] from the Tower,
10　　And was embarked to cross to Burgundy,
　　And in my company my brother Gloucester,
　　Who from my cabin tempted[5] me to walk
　　Upon the hatches.[6] There we looked toward England,
　　And cited[7] up a thousand heavy times,
15　　During the wars of York and Lancaster,
　　That had befall'n us. As we paced along
　　Upon the giddy[8] footing of the hatches,
　　Methought that Gloucester stumbled, and in falling
　　Struck me (that thought to stay him) overboard,

1 jailor
2 sluggish, draggy
3 it seemed★
4 escaped
5 induced
6 deck
7 called
8 staggery, dizzy, whirling★

Into the tumbling billows[9] of the main.[10]   20
O Lord, methought what pain it was to drown,
What dreadful noise of waters in mine ears!
What sights of ugly death within mine eyes.
Methoughts I saw a thousand fearful wracks,[11]
A thousand men that fishes gnawed upon,   25
Wedges[12] of gold, great anchors, heaps of pearl,
Inestimable stones,[13] unvalued[14] jewels,
All scattered in the bottom of the sea.
Some lay in dead men's skulls, and in those holes
Where eyes did once inhabit,[15] there were crept,   30
As 'twere in scorn of eyes, reflecting gems,
Which wooed[16] the slimy bottom of the deep,
And mocked the dead bones that lay scattered by.[17]

Keeper   Had you such leisure in the time of death
     To gaze upon the secrets of the deep?   35

Clarence Methought I had, and often did I strive
     To yield the ghost,[18] but still the envious flood[19]
     Stopped in[20] my soul, and would not let it forth
     To seek the empty, vast, and wand'ring air,

---

 9 swelling waves
10 sea
11 wrecked ships
12 ingots
13 inestimable stones = uncountable numbers of precious stones
   (inEStiMAHble)
14 incredibly / extremely valuable
15 reside
16 courted, called to
17 and MOCKED the DEAD bones THAT lay SCAterred BY
18 yield the ghost = die ("give up the spirit of life")
19 (1) water, (2) stream★
20 stopped in = plugged up, closed in★

40   But smothered it within my panting bulk,[21]
     Who[22] almost burst to belch[23] it in the sea.
     Keeper   Awaked you not in this sore agony?
     Clarence No, no, my dream was lengthened after life.
     O then began the tempest to my soul.
45   I passed, methought, the melancholy flood,
     With[24] that sour ferryman[25] which poets write of,
     Unto[26] the kingdom of perpetual night.[27]
     The first that there did greet my stranger[28] soul
     Was my great father-in-law, renownèd Warwick,
50   Who spake aloud, "What scourge[29] for perjury[30]
     Can this dark monarchy afford false Clarence?"
     And so[31] he vanished. Then came wand'ring by
     A shadow[32] like an angel, with bright hair
     Dabbled[33] in blood, and he shrieked out aloud,
55   "Clarence is come, false, fleeting, perjured Clarence,
     That stabbed me in the field by Tewkesbury!
     Seize on him, furies, take him unto torment!"
     With that methought a legion of foul fiends

21 body
22 I who
23 emit, eject
24 by means of
25 sour ferryman = bitter/harsh/gloomy Charon, who took newly dead souls
   across the River Styx
26 passed . . . unto
27 Hades, Hell
28 alien, foreign ("non-native")
29 punishment
30 violating a vow/oath
31 then, thereafter
32 ghost (Edward, Prince of Wales, Henry VI's son)
33 stained, splashed

Environed[34] me, and howlèd in mine ears
Such hideous cries, that with the very noise   60
I trembling waked, and for a season[35] after
Could not believe but that I was in hell,
Such terrible impression[36] made my dream.

Keeper   No marvel, lord, though[37] it affrighted you.
I am afraid (methinks) to hear you tell it.   65

Clarence   Ah Keeper, Keeper, I have done these things,
Which now give evidence against my soul,
For Edward's sake, and see how he requites me.
O God! If my deep prayers cannot appease thee,
But thou wilt be avenged on my misdeeds,   70
Yet execute thy wrath in[38] me alone.
O spare my guiltless wife, and my poor children.
Keeper, I prithee[39] sit by me awhile.
My soul is heavy, and I fain would[40] sleep.

Keeper   I will, my lord, God give your Grace good rest.   75

CLARENCE SLEEPS

ENTER BRAKENBURY

Brakenbury Sorrow breaks[41] seasons and reposing[42] hours,
Makes the night morning, and the noontide night.

34 encircled
35 period★
36 effect
37 that
38 on
39 pray thee★
40 fain would = would be glad to
41 shatters, dissolves
42 resting

Princes have but their titles for their glories,

An outward honor for an inward toil,

80 And for unfelt[43] imaginations[44]

They often feel a world of restless cares.

So that between their titles, and low[45] name,

There's nothing differs but the outward fame.[46]

ENTER THE TWO MURDERERS

Murderer 1   Ho, who's here?

85 *Brakenbury*   What would'st thou, fellow? And how cam'st thou
hither?

Murderer 1   I would speak with Clarence, and I came hither on
my legs.

Brakenbury   What, so brief?

Murderer 2   'Tis better, sir, than to be tedious.[47]
Show him our commission, and talk no more.

90 *Brakenbury*   (*reads*) "I am in this commanded to deliver
The noble Duke of Clarence to your hands."
I will not reason[48] what is meant hereby,
Because I will[49] be guiltless from the meaning.
There lies the Duke asleep, and there the keys.

95 I'll to the King, and signify[50] to him
That thus I have resigned[51] to you my charge.

43 non-palpable/physical
44 iMAdjiNAYseeOWNZ
45 humble
46 talk
47 prolix, wearisome★
48 question, discuss★
49 wish to
50 make known★
51 surrendered★

Murderer 1   You may, sir, 'tis a point[52] of wisdom.
Fare you well.

EXEUNT BRAKENBURY AND KEEPER

Murderer 2   What, shall we stab him as he sleeps?

Murderer 1   No. He'll say 'twas done cowardly, when he wakes.   100

Murderer 2   Why, he shall never wake until the great Judgment Day.

Murderer 1   Why, then he will say we stabbed him sleeping.

Murderer 2   The urging[53] of that word "judgment" hath bred a kind of remorse in me.   105

Murderer 1   What? Art thou afraid?

Murderer 2   Not to kill him, having a warrant, but to be damned for killing him, from the which no warrant can defend[54] me.

Murderer 1   I thought thou hadst been resolute.

Murderer 2   So I am, to let him live.   110

Murderer 1   I'll back to the Duke of Gloucester, and tell him so.

Murderer 2   Nay, I prithee, stay a little. I hope this passionate[55] humor of mine will change, it was wont to hold me[56] but while one tells[57] twenty.

Murderer 1   How dost thou feel thyself now?   115

Murderer 2   Some certain dregs of conscience are yet within me.

Murderer 1   Remember our reward, when the deed's done.

Murderer 2   Come, he dies. I had forgot the reward.

Murderer 1   Where's thy conscience now?

52 mark
53 presenting
54 protect★
55 compassionate
56 was wont to hold me = usually★ keeps/lasts★ me
57 counts

120 *Murderer 2* O, in the Duke of Gloucester's purse.

    Murderer 1 When he opens his purse to give us our reward, thy
        conscience flies out?

    Murderer 2 'Tis no matter, let it go. There's few or none will
        entertain it.

125 *Murderer 1* How if it come to thee again?

    Murderer 2 I'll not meddle[58] with it, it makes a man a coward. A
        man cannot steal, but it accuseth him. A man cannot swear,
        but it checks[59] him. A man cannot lie with his neighbor's
        wife, but it detects him. 'Tis a blushing shamefaced spirit that
130   mutinies in a man's bosom. It fills a man full of obstacles. It
        made me once restore a purse of gold that (by chance) I
        found. It beggars any man that keeps it. It is turned out of
        towns and cities for a dangerous thing, and every man that
        means to live well endeavors to trust to himself and to live
135   without it.

    Murderer 1 'Tis even now at my elbow, persuading me not to kill
        the Duke.

    Murderer 2 Take[60] the devil in thy mind, and believe him not.
        He would insinuate with[61] thee but[62] to make thee sigh.

140 *Murderer 1* I am strong-framed, he cannot prevail with me.

    Murderer 2 Spoke like a tall[63] man that respects his reputation.
        Come, shall we fall to work?

    Murderer 1 Take him on the costard[64] with the hilts of thy

58 associate, join
59 stops★
60 admit, receive, allow
61 insinuate with = worm himself/sneak into
62 only
63 proper
64 head (costard = a form of apple)

sword, and then throw him in the malmsey-butt[65] in the
next room.   145

Murderer 2	O excellent device![66] And make a sop[67] of him.
Murderer 1	Soft, he wakes.
Murderer 2	Strike.
Murderer 1	No, we'll reason with him.
Clarence	Where art thou, Keeper? Give me a cup of wine.

150

Murderer 2	You shall have wine enough my lord, anon.[68]
Clarence	In God's name, what art thou?
Murderer 2	A man, as you are.
Clarence	But not, as I am, royal.
Murderer 2	Nor you, as we are, loyal.

155

Clarence	Thy voice is thunder, but thy looks are humble.
Murderer 2	My voice is now the King's, my looks mine own.
Clarence	How darkly and how deadly dost thou speak.

Your eyes do menace me. Why look you pale?

Who sent you hither? Wherefore[69] do you come?   160

Both Murderers	To, to, to –
Clarence	To murder me?
Both Murderers	Aye, aye.
Clarence	You scarcely have the hearts to tell me so,

And therefore cannot have the hearts to do it.   165

Wherein, my friends, have I offended you?

Murderer 1	Offended us you have not, but the King.
Clarence	I shall be reconciled to him again.

65 cask of strong sweet wine, holding over 100 gallons
66 scheme, plan
67 bread soaked in wine before eating
68 right away, very soon★
69 why★

    Murderer 2 Never my lord, therefore prepare to die.

170 *Clarence*   Are you drawn forth from among a world of men

        To slay the innocent? What is my offense?

        Where is the evidence that doth accuse me?

        What lawful quest[70] have given their verdict up

        Unto the frowning judge? Or who pronounced

175   The bitter sentence of poor Clarence's death?

        Before I be convict[71] by course of law,

        To threaten me with death is most unlawful.

        I charge you, as you hope to have redemption

        By Christ's dear blood shed for our grievous sins,

180   That you depart and lay no hands on me.

        The deed you undertake is damnable.

    Murderer 1 What we will do, we do upon command.

    Murderer 2 And he that hath commanded is our King.

    Clarence   Erroneous vassals,[72] the great King of kings

185   Hath in the tables[73] of his law commanded

        That thou shalt do no murder. Will you then

        Spurn at his edict and fulfill a man's?[74]

        Take heed. For he holds vengeance in his hand,

        To hurl upon their heads that break his law.

190 *Murderer 2* And that same vengeance doth he hurl on thee,

        For false forswearing, and for murder too.

        Thou didst receive the sacrament, to fight

        In quarrel of the house of Lancaster.

---

70 inquest
71 pronounced guilt, convicted (kanVICT)
72 erroneous vassals = misguided subordinates★
73 tablets
74 fulfill a man's = effect/complete the verdict of a mere man

Murderer 1   And like a traitor to the name of God,

    Didst break that vow; and with thy treacherous blade   195

    Unrip'st[75] the bowels of thy sovereign's son.

Murderer 2   Whom thou wast sworn to cherish and defend.

Murderer 1   How canst thou urge God's dreadful law to us,

    When thou hast broke it in such dear degree?[76]

Clarence   Alas! For whose sake did I that ill deed?   200

    For Edward, for my brother, for his sake.

    He sends you not to murder me for this,

    For in that sin he is as deep as I.

    If God will be avengèd for the deed,

    O know you yet, he[77] doth it publicly,   205

    Take not the quarrel from his powerful arm.

    He needs no indirect nor lawless course

    To cut off those that have offended him.

Murderer 1   Who made thee, then, a bloody minister,

    When gallant-springing[78] brave Plantagenet,   210

    That princely novice, was struck dead by thee?[79]

Clarence   My brother's love, the devil, and my rage.

Murderer 1   Thy brother's love, our duty, and thy faults,[80]

    Provoke[81] us hither now to slaughter thee.

Clarence   If you do love my brother, hate not me.   215

    I am his brother, and I love him well.

    If you are hired for meed, go back again,

75 laid open
76 dear degree = grievous/dire manner/way
77 God
78 gallant-springing = growing more and more handsome
79 that PRINCEly NOvice WAS struck DEAD by THEE
80 transgressions, offenses
81 call, summon

And I will send you to my brother Gloucester,

Who shall reward you better for my life

220 Than Edward will for tidings of my death.

Murderer 2 You are deceived, your brother Gloucester

hates you.

Clarence O no, he loves me, and he holds me dear.

Go you to him from me.

Both Murderers   Aye, so we will.

Clarence Tell him, when that our princely father York

225 Blessed his three sons with his victorious arm,

He little thought of this divided[82] friendship.

Bid Gloucester think of this, and he will weep.

Murderer 1 Aye, millstones, as he lessoned[83] us to weep.

Clarence O do not slander him, for he is kind.

230 *Murderer 1* Right, as snow in harvest.

Come, you deceive yourself,

'Tis he that sends us to destroy you here.

Clarence It cannot be, for he bewept my fortune,

And hugged me in his arms, and swore with sobs

235 That he would labor[84] my delivery.

Murderer 1 Why so he doth, when he delivers thee

From this world's thralldom[85] to the joys of heaven.

Murderer 2 Make peace with God, for you must die, my lord.

Clarence Hast thou that holy feeling in thy soul

240 To counsel me to make my peace with God,

And art thou yet to thy own soul so blind,

82 separated★
83 instructed, admonished
84 strive / work for
85 bondage, servitude

That thou wilt war with God by murdering me?

O sirs, consider, they that set you on

To do this deed will hate you for the deed.

Murderer 2 What shall we do?

Clarence   Relent,[86] and save your souls.   245

Which of you, if you were a prince's son,

Being pent from liberty, as I am now,

If two such murderers as yourselves came to you,

Would not entreat for life?

Murderer 1 Relent? No. 'Tis cowardly and womanish.[87]   250

Clarence   Not to relent is beastly, savage, divilish.[88]

My friend, I spy some pity in thy looks.

O, if thine eye be not a flatterer,

Come thou on my side, and entreat[89] for me.[90]

A begging prince what beggar pities not?   255

Murderer 2 Look behind you, my lord.

Murderer 1 (*stabbing him*) Take that, and that. If all this will
not do,

I'll drown you in the malmsey-butt within.[91]

MURDERER I EXITS, WITH THE BODY

Murderer 2 A bloody deed, and desperately[92] dispatched.

How fain, like Pilate,[93] would I wash my hands   260

86 abandon/give up this murder

87 reLENT no 'tis COWardLY and WOmaNISH

88 devilish (perhaps bi- rather than trisyllabic)

89 plead, negotiate★

90 come THOU on MY side AND enTREAT for ME

91 inside

92 despairingly, hopelessly★

93 Pontius Pilate, Roman governor of Judea when Christ was crucified

Of this most grievous murder.

ENTER MURDERER 1

Murderer 1 How now? What mean'st thou, that thou help'st
me not?

By heaven, the Duke shall know how slack you have been.

Murderer 2 I would he knew that I had saved his brother.

265 Take thou the fee, and tell him what I say;

For I repent me that the Duke is slain.

EXIT MURDERER 2

Murderer 1 So do not I. Go, coward as thou art.

Well, I'll go hide the body in some hole,

Till that the Duke give order for his burial.

270 And when I have my meed,[94] I will away,

For this will out, and then I must not stay.

EXIT

94 wages, reward

Act 2

SCENE I

London, The palace

FLOURISH

ENTER KING EDWARD IV, SICK, QUEEN ELIZABETH, DORSET,
RIVERS, HASTINGS, BUCKINGHAM, GREY, AND OTHERS

Edward Why so. Now have I done a good day's work.
  You peers,[1] continue this united league.[2]
  I every day expect[3] an embassage[4]
  From my Redeemer to redeem me hence.
  And more to peace my soul shall part[5] to heaven,   5
  Since I have made my friends at peace on earth.
  Rivers and Hastings, take each other's hand,
  Dissemble not your hatred, swear your love.

---

1 noblemen
2 covenant, alliance★
3 await★
4 ambassadorial message
5 leave, go away

Rivers   By heaven, my heart is purged from grudging[6] hate,

10   And with my hand I seal[7] my true heart's love.

Hastings So thrive I,[8] as I truly swear the like.[9]

Edward   Take heed you dally[10] not before your king,

Lest he that is the supreme[11] King of kings

Confound[12] your hidden falsehood, and award[13]

15   Either of you to be the other's end.

Hastings So prosper I, as I swear perfect love!

Rivers   And I, as I love Hastings with my heart!

Edward   Madam, yourself is not exempt from this,

Nor you, son Dorset – Buckingham, nor you.

20   You have been factious one against the other.

Wife, love Lord Hastings, let him kiss your hand,

And what you do, do it unfeignedly.[14]

Elizabeth (*offering her hand*) There, Hastings, I will never more remember

Our former hatred, so thrive I and mine![15]

25   *Edward*   Dorset, embrace him. Hastings, love Lord Marquess.[16]

Dorset   This interchange of love, I here protest,

Upon my part shall be inviolable.[17]

Hastings   And so swear I.

6 resentful, unwilling
7 attest to
8 may I prosper/succeed★
9 same
10 trifle, fool about★
11 SOOpreem
12 demolish, destroy, corrupt★
13 appoint
14 sincerely, honestly ("without pretense")
15 our FORmer HAtred SO thrive I and MINE
16 Dorset
17 sacredly free from violation (inVIEaLAYble)

THEY EMBRACE

Edward   Now, princely Buckingham, seal thou this league

    With thy embracements to my wife's allies,   30

    And make me happy in your unity.

Buckingham (*to Elizabeth*) Whenever Buckingham doth turn

    his hate

    Upon your Grace, but[18] with all duteous love

    Doth cherish you, and yours, God punish me

    With hate in those where I expect most love.   35

    When I have most need to employ a friend,

    And most assurèd that he is a friend,[19]

    Deep, hollow,[20] treacherous, and full of guile

    Be he unto me! This do I beg of heaven,[21]

    When I am cold in love, to you or yours.   40

Edward   A pleasing cordial,[22] princely Buckingham,

    Is this thy vow unto my sickly heart.

    There wanteth now our brother Gloucester here,[23]

    To make the blessèd period of this peace.

Buckingham And in good time,   45

    Here comes Sir Richard Ratcliff, and the Duke.

ENTER GLOUCESTER AND RATCLIFF

Gloucester   Good morrow[24] to my sovereign king and queen,

18 rather than
19 and MOST asSURed THAT he IS a FRIEND
20 deep, hollow = secretive, false
21 be HE unTO me THIS do I BEG of HEAVEN ("heaven" = often
   shortened to a monosyllable)
22 comfort, restorative
23 to be here
24 morning

And princely peers, a happy time of day.

Edward   Happy, indeed, as we[25] have spent the day.

50   Gloucester, we done deeds of charity,

Made peace[26] enmity, fair love of hate,

Between these swelling[27] wrong-incensèd[28] peers.

Gloucester A blessèd labor, my most sovereign lord.

Among this princely heap,[29] if any here

55   By false intelligence,[30] or wrong surmise,

Hold me a foe —

If I unwittingly, or in my rage

Have aught committed that is hardly[31] borne

By any in this presence, I desire

60   To reconcile me to his friendly peace.

'Tis death to me to be at enmity.

I hate it, and desire all good men's love.

First, madam, I entreat true peace of you,

Which I will purchase with my duteous service.

65   Of you, my noble cousin Buckingham,

If ever any grudge were lodged between us —

Of you and you, Lord Rivers and of Dorset

That all without desert have frowned on me —

Dukes, earls, lords, gentlemen — indeed, of all.[32]

70   I do not know that Englishman alive

25 I
26 peace into
27 proud
28 wrong-incensèd = (1) inflamed by wrongs, (2) wrongly inflamed
29 company, group
30 understanding, knowledge, information
31 painfully
32 dukes EARLS lords GENtilMEN inDEED of ALL

With whom my soul is any jot[33] at odds
More than the[34] infant that is[35] born tonight.
I thank my God for my humility.

Elizabeth   A holy day shall this be kept hereafter.
I would to God all strifes were well compounded.[36]   75
My sovereign lord, I do beseech your Highness
To take our brother Clarence to your Grace.

Gloucester   Why madam, have I offered love for this –
To be so flouted[37] in this royal presence?
Who knows not that the gentle Duke is dead?   80

ALL ARE VISIBLY STARTLED

You do him injury to scorn his corse.

Rivers   Who knows not he is dead?! Who knows he is?

Elizabeth   All-seeing heaven, what a world is this!

Buckingham   Look I so pale, Lord Dorset, as the rest?[38]

Dorset   Aye, my good lord, and no man in the presence   85
But his red color hath forsook his cheeks.

Edward   Is Clarence dead? The order was reversed.[39]

Gloucester   But he (poor man) by your first order died,
And that[40] a wingèd Mercury[41] did bear.
Some tardy[42] cripple bore the countermand,[43]   90

33 smallest bit
34 an, any
35 will be
36 settled
37 mocked, insulted, jeered at★
38 rest of you
39 revoked, annulled
40 that order
41 messenger of the gods
42 slow, sluggish, dilatory★
43 annulment

That came too lag,[44] to see him buried.

God grant[45] that some, less noble and less loyal,

Nearer[46] in bloody thoughts, but not in blood,

Deserve not worse than wretched Clarence did,

95   And yet go current[47] from suspicion!

ENTER STANLEY

Stanley (*kneeling*) A boon, my sovereign, for my service done.[48]

Edward I prithee peace,[49] my soul is full of sorrow.

Stanley I will not rise, unless your Highness grant.

Edward Then say at once what is it thou requests.

100 *Stanley* The forfeit, sovereign, of my servant's life,[50]

Who slew today a riotous[51] gentleman

Lately attendant on the Duke of Norfolk.

Edward Have I a tongue to doom[52] my brother's death,

And shall that tongue give pardon to a slave?

105   My brother killed no man, his fault was thought,

And yet his punishment was bitter death.

Who sued to me for him? Who (in my wrath)

Kneeled at my feet and bid me be advised?

Who spoke of brotherhood? Who spoke of love?

44 late
45 knows
46 more like, closer* to him
47 (1) freely along ("flowing"), (2) accepted
48 i.e., for services rendered, *not* for a specific service
49 I prithee peace = please don't bother me now
50 i.e., "the forfeited life of my servant": by committing a capital crime, the
   servant had forfeited his life to the King, and Stanley asks that it be
   transferred, instead, to him
51 wanton, quarrelsome, drunken
52 pronounce

Who told me how the poor soul[53] did forsake   110
The mighty Warwick, and did fight for me?
Who told me[54] in the field by Tewkesbury,
When Oxford had me down, he rescued me,
And said, "Dear brother, live, and be a king"?
Who told me, when we both lay in the field   115
Frozen almost to death, how he did lap[55] me
Even in his own garments, and did give himself,[56]
All thin[57] and naked, to the numb[58] cold night?
All this from my remembrance brutish wrath
Sinfully plucked, and not a man of you   120
Had so much grace to put it in my mind.
But when your carters,[59] or your waiting vassals
Have done a drunken slaughter, and defaced[60]
The precious image[61] of our dear Redeemer,[62]
You straight are on your knees for pardon, pardon,   125
And I (unjustly too) must grant it you.
But for my brother not a man would speak,
Nor I, ungracious, speak unto myself
For him, poor soul. The proudest of you all
Have been beholding[63] to him in his life.   130

53 person, man (Clarence)
54 told me = mentioned/reminded me
55 wrap
56 even [often shortened to a monosyllable] in HIS own GARments AND did
    GIVE himSELF
57 thinly/lightly clad
58 numbing
59 cart drivers
60 disfigured, destroyed
61 likeness, representation ("picture")★
62 i.e., in whose likeness we are all made
63 beholden, under obligation★

Yet none of you would once plead for his life.[64]
O God, I fear thy justice will take hold
On me, and you, and mine, and yours for this!
Come Hastings, help me to my closet.[65]

135 Ah poor Clarence!

EXEUNT SOME WITH EDWARD AND ELIZABETH

Gloucester   This is the fruits of rashness. Mark you not
How that the guilty kindred of the Queen
Looked pale, when they did hear of Clarence's death?
O, they did urge it still[66] unto the King!

140 God will revenge it. Come lords, will you go
To comfort Edward with our company?

Buckingham We wait upon your Grace.

EXEUNT

64 yet NONE of YOU would ONCE plead FOR his LIFE
65 private room
66 always

SCENE 2

The palace

<small>ENTER DUCHESS OF YORK, WITH CLARENCE'S TWO CHILDREN</small>

Boy	Good grandam tell us, is our father dead?
Duchess of York	No, boy.
Girl	Why do you weep so oft, and beat your breast,
	And cry, "O Clarence, my unhappy son!"
Boy	Why do you look on us, and shake your head, 5
	And call us orphans, wretches, castaways
	If that our noble father were alive?
Duchess of York	My pretty cousins,[1] you mistake me both,
	I do lament the sickness of the King,
	As loath to lose him, not your father's death. 10
	It were lost sorrow to wail one that's lost.
Boy	Then you conclude, my grandam, he is dead.
	The King my uncle is to blame for it.
	God will revenge it, whom I will importune
	With earnest prayers, all to that effect. 15
Girl	And so will I.
Duchess of York	Peace children, peace! The King doth love you well.
	Incapable and shallow[2] innocents,
	You cannot guess who caused your father's death.
Boy	Grandam, we can, for my good uncle Gloucester 20
	Told me the King, provoked to it by the Queen,
	Devised impeachments[3] to imprison him,

---

1 kindred, relatives
2 incapable and shallow = unfit and inexperienced/lacking weight★
3 devised impeachments = arranged/contrived★ accusations/charges

And when my uncle told me so, he wept,

And pitied me, and kindly kissed my cheek,

25　　Bade me rely on him as on my father,

And he would love me dearly as a child.

Duchess of York　Ah! That deceit should steal such gentle shape,

And with a virtuous vizor[4] hide deep vice!

He is my son, aye, and therein my shame,

30　　Yet from my dugs[5] he drew not this deceit.

Boy　　　　　Think you my uncle did dissemble, grandam?

Duchess of York　Aye, boy.

Boy　　　　　I cannot think it. Hark,[6] what noise is this?

ENTER ELIZABETH, WITH HER HAIR ABOUT HER EARS,
RIVERS AND DORSET AFTER HER

Elizabeth　　　Ah! Who shall hinder[7] me to wail and weep,

35　　To chide[8] my fortune, and torment myself?

I'll join with black despair against my soul,

And to myself become an enemy.

Duchess of York　What means this scene of rude impatience?[9]

Elizabeth　　　To make[10] an act of tragic violence.

40　　Edward, my lord, your son, our king, is dead.

Why grow the branches when the root is gone?

Why wither not the leaves that want their sap?

If you will live, lament. If die, be brief,

4 the face covering of a battle helmet
5 breasts ("nipples")
6 listen★
7 stop, prevent
8 give vent to displeasure, scold
9 rude impatience = ignorant/barbarous failure of endurance/tolerance of
suffering
10 match, frame, represent

That[11] our swift-winged souls may catch the King's,
Or like obedient subjects follow him   45
To his new kingdom of perpetual rest.

Duchess of York Ah, so much interest[12] have I in thy sorrow
As I had title[13] in thy noble husband.
I have bewept a worthy husband's death,
And lived with[14] looking on his images.   50
But now two mirrors of his[15] princely semblance[16]
Are cracked in pieces by malignant[17] death,
And I for comfort have but one false glass,[18]
Which grieves me when I see my shame in him.
Thou art a widow, yet thou art a mother,   55
And hast the comfort of thy children left,
But death hath snatched my husband from mine arms
And plucked two crutches[19] from my feeble hands,
Clarence and Edward. O, what cause have I
(Thine being but a moiety of my grief)   60
To overgo thy plaints and drown thy cries!

Boy   Ah aunt! You wept not for our father's death.
How can we aid you with our kindred tears?

Girl   Our fatherless distress[20] was left unmoaned,

11 so that
12 share, claim
13 rank, honor
14 by means of
15 her husband's
16 likeness
17 virulent, evil
18 Gloucester
19 props, supports
20 affliction★

65 Your widow-dolor[21] likewise be unwept.

Elizabeth Give me no help in lamentation,
I am not barren to bring forth complaints.[22]
All springs reduce[23] their currents to mine eyes,
That[24] I, being governed by the watery moon,[25]

70 May send forth plenteous tears to drown the world!
Ah, for my husband, for my dear Lord Edward!

Children Ah, for our father, for our dear Lord Clarence!

Duchess of York Alas for both, both mine, Edward and Clarence!

Elizabeth What stay[26] had I but Edward, and he's gone.

75 *Children* What stay had we but Clarence? And he's gone.

Duchess of York What stays had I but they? And they are gone.

Elizabeth Was never widow had so dear[27] a loss!

Children Were never orphans had so dear a loss!

Duchess of York Was never mother had so dear a loss!

80 Alas, I am the mother of these griefs,
Their woes are parceled,[28] mine are general.[29]
She for an Edward weeps, and so do I.
I for a Clarence weep, so doth not she.
These babes for Clarence weep, and so do I.

85 I for an Edward weep, so do not they.
Alas! You three, on me threefold distressed,
Pour all your tears, I am your sorrow's nurse,

21 suffering, distress
22 grieving, lamentations
23 lead
24 so that
25 i.e., female
26 strength
27 precious, rare
28 (1) divided, (2) particular
29 undivided, all-embracing, universal★

And I will pamper it with lamentation.

Dorset   (*to Elizabeth*) Comfort, dear mother, God is
much displeased

That you take with unthankfulness his doing.   90

In common worldly things, 'tis called ungrateful,

With dull unwillingness to repay a debt

Which with a bounteous hand was kindly lent.

Much more to be thus opposite with[30] heaven,

For it requires[31] the royal debt it lent you.   95

Rivers   Madam, bethink you like a careful mother

Of the young Prince your son. Send straight for him,

Let him be crowned. In him your comfort lives.

Drown desperate sorrow in dead Edward's grave,

And plant your joys in living Edward's throne.   100

ENTER GLOUCESTER, BUCKINGHAM, STANLEY,
HASTINGS, AND RATCLIFF

Gloucester   Sister, have comfort, all of us have cause

To wail the dimming of our shining star.

But none can help our harms by wailing them.

Madam, my mother, I do cry you mercy,

I did not see your Grace. Humbly on my knee   105

I crave your blessing.

Duchess of York God bless thee, and put meekness in thy breast,

Love, charity, obedience, and true duty.

Gloucester   (*aside*) Amen, and make me die a good old man.

That is the butt-end[32] of a mother's blessing,   110

30 opposite with = opposed/contrary/antagonistic★ to
31 requests, commands, desires
32 butt-end = concluding part

I marvel that her Grace did leave it out.

Buckingham   You cloudy[33] princes, and heart-sorrowing
peers,

That bear this mutual heavy load of moan,

Now cheer[34] each other in each other's love.

115   Though we have spent our harvest of this king,

We are to reap the harvest of his son.

The broken rancor[35] of your high-swoll'n hates,

But lately splintered,[36] knit, and joined together,

Must gently be preserved, cherished, and kept.

120   Me seemeth good, that, with some little train,[37]

Forthwith from Ludlow the young Prince be fet[38]

Hither to London, to be crowned our king.

Rivers   Why with some little train, my Lord of
Buckingham?

Buckingham   Marry my lord, lest by a multitude

125   The new-healed wound of malice should break out,

Which would be so much the more dangerous

By[39] how much the estate[40] is green and yet ungoverned.[41]

Where[42] every horse bears his[43] commanding rein,

And may direct[44] his course as please himself,

33 gloomy, frowning
34 comfort, console
35 broken rancor = shattered/ruptured/fragmented grudges/animosities
36 splinted, bound up
37 escort, retainers, attendants
38 fetched
39 because of
40 state, condition★
41 uncontrolled★
42 in a situation where
43 his own/separate
44 control, regulate, order★

As well the fear of harm as harm apparent,[45]   130
In my opinion, ought to be prevented.

Gloucester   I hope[46] the King made peace with all of us,
And the compact[47] is firm and true in me.

Rivers   And so in me, and so (I think) in all.
Yet since it is but green, it should be put   135
To no apparent likelihood of breach,
Which haply[48] by much company might be urged.
Therefore I say with noble Buckingham,
That it is meet[49] so few should fetch the Prince.

Hastings   And so say I.   140

Gloucester   Then be it so, and go we to determine
Who they shall be that straight shall post to Ludlow.
Madam, and you, my sister, will you go
To give your censures[50] in this weighty business?

Duchess of York With all our hearts.   145

EXEUNT ALL BUT BUCKINGHAM AND GLOUCESTER

Buckingham   My lord, whoever journeys to the Prince,
For God's sake, let not us two stay at home.
For by the way, I'll sort occasion[51]
(As index[52] to the story[53] we late talked of)

---

45 appearing, showing itself
46 trust, expect
47 covenant, agreement
48 perhaps★
49 proper, appropriate★
50 opinions, judgments
51 sort occasion = arrange/manage★ circumstances/opportunity★
52 as index = in token/accordance with★
53 plot ("narrative/sequence of events")

150   To part[54] the Queen's proud kindred from the Prince.

    Gloucester My other self, my counsel's consistory,[55]

        My oracle,[56] my prophet, my dear cousin.

        I, as[57] a child, will go by thy direction.[58]

        Toward Ludlow then, for we'll not stay behind.

EXEUNT

54 separate★
55 council, seat of authority
56 mouthpiece of the gods, vehicle of divine communication
57 as if
58 instruction, guidance★

SCENE 3

London, A street

ENTER A CITIZEN[1] FROM ONE END OF THE STAGE,
AND ANOTHER FROM THE OPPOSITE SIDE

Citizen 1 Good morrow, neighbor, whither away so fast?

Citizen 2 I promise you, I scarcely know myself
Hear you the news abroad?

Citizen 1 Yes, that the King is dead.

Citizen 2 Bad news, by'r lady.[2] Seldom comes the better.[3]   5
I fear, I fear 'twill prove a giddy world.

ENTER A THIRD CITIZEN

Citizen 3 Neighbors, God speed![4]

Citizen 1 Give[5] you good morrow, sir.

Citizen 3 Doth the news hold,[6] of good King Edward's death?

Citizen 2 Aye sir, it is too true, God help the while.[7]   10

Citizen 3 Then masters,[8] look to see a troublous[9] world.

Citizen 1 No, no, by God's good grace his son shall reign.

Citizen 3 Woe to that land that's governed by a child!

Citizen 2 In him there is a hope of government,[10]

1 a man possessing civic rights and privileges, by virtue of his economic
standing, a burgess (England did not grant universal male suffrage until the
19th c.)★
2 by'r lady = by Mary mother of God
3 the better = the better kind of news
4 God speed = may God make you prosper★
5 I give
6 stand up
7 day, time
8 term of address used for people below gentlemanly rank
9 unsettled, disturbed, agitated
10 control, authority

15   That in his nonage council[11] under him,

And in his full and ripened years himself,

No doubt shall then, and till then, govern well.

Citizen 1 So stood the state when Henry the Sixth

Was crowned in Paris, but at nine months old.

20 *Citizen 3* Stood the state so? No, no, good friends, God wot,[12]

For then this land was famously[13] enriched

With politic grave[14] counsel. Then the King

Had virtuous uncles to protect his Grace.

Citizen 1 Why so hath this, both by his father and mother.

25 *Citizen 3* Better it were they all came by his father,

Or[15] by his father there were none at all.[16]

For emulation,[17] who shall now be nearest,[18]

Will touch us all too near,[19] if God prevent not.

O full of danger is the Duke of Gloucester,

30   And the Queen's sons and brothers, haught[20] and proud.

And were they to be ruled, and not to rule,

This sickly land might solace[21] as before.

Citizen 1 Come, come, we fear the worst. All will be well.

Citizen 3 When clouds appear, wise men put on their cloaks.

35   When great leaves fall, then winter is at hand.

---

11 a group of noble advisers
12 knows
13 wonderfully*
14 politic grave = prudent/sagacious/shrewd respected/sober
15 or else ("either that or")
16 i.e., unity/consistency of judgment is crucial
17 rivalry, contention
18 closest to power
19 closely
20 haughty, arrogant
21 be comforted/consoled

When the sun sets, who doth not look for night?
Untimely storms make men expect a dearth.
All may be well, but if God sort it so,
'Tis more than we deserve, or I expect.

Citizen 2 Truly, the souls of men are full of fear.   40
You cannot reason (almost) with a man
That looks not heavily, and full of dread.

Citizen 3 Before the days of change, still[22] is it so.
By a divine instinct, men's minds mistrust
Pursuing danger,[23] as by proof we see   45
The water swell before a boisterous[24] storm.
But leave it all to God. Whither away?

Citizen 2 Marry, we were sent for to the justices.[25]

Citizen 3 And so was I. I'll bear[26] you company.

EXEUNT

22 always
23 pursuing danger = danger that is coming/following (Quarto: ensuing
   danger)
24 rough, massive, violent
25 judges
26 keep

SCENE 4

London, The palace

ENTER ARCHBISHOP OF YORK, RICHARD (DUKE OF YORK),
QUEEN ELIZABETH, AND THE DUCHESS OF YORK

Archbishop   Last night I heard they lay[1] at Stony Stratford,
   And at Northampton they do rest tonight.
   Tomorrow, or next day, they will be here.
Duchess of York I long with all my heart to see the Prince.[2]
5 I hope he is much grown since last I saw him.
Elizabeth   But I hear, no, they say my son[3] of York
   Has almost overta'en him in his growth.
York   Aye mother, but I would not have it so.[4]
Duchess of York Why, my young cousin, it is good to grow.
10 *York*   Grandam, one night, as we did sit at supper,
   My uncle Rivers talked how I did grow
   More than my brother. "Aye," quoth[5] my uncle Gloucester,
   "Small herbs[6] have grace, great weeds[7] do grow apace."[8]
   And since[9] methinks I would not grow so fast,
15 Because sweet flowers are slow, and weeds make haste.
Duchess of York Good faith, good faith, the saying did not hold
   In him[10] that did object the same to thee.

---

1 slept, rested
2 Edward, Prince of Wales (York's older brother)
3 i.e., her stepson
4 would not have it = do not wish it
5 said★
6 soft-stemmed useful plants
7 non-useful plants, growing where they are not wanted
8 rapidly
9 since then
10 Gloucester, her son

He was the wretched'st thing when he was young,
So long a-growing, and so leisurely,
That if this rule were true, he should[11] be gracious.   20

Archbishop of York   And so no doubt he is, my gracious madam.

Duchess of York   I hope he is, but yet let mothers doubt.

York   Now by my troth, if I had been
remembered,[12]
    I could have given my uncle's grace a flout,
    To touch his growth nearer than he touched mine.   25

Duchess of York   How, my young York? I prithee let me hear it.

York   Marry, they say my uncle grew so fast
    That he could gnaw a crust at two hours old.
    'Twas full two years ere I could get a tooth.
    Grandam, this would have been a biting jest.   30

Duchess of York   I pray thee, pretty York, who told thee this?

York   Grandam, his nurse.

Duchess of York   His nurse? Why she was dead ere thou wast
    born.

York   If 'twere not she, I cannot tell who told me.

Elizabeth   A parlous[13] boy. Go to,[14] you are too   35
shrewd.[15]

Archbishop of York   Good madam, be not angry with the child.

Elizabeth   Pitchers have ears.

ENTER A MESSENGER

11 ought to
12 been remembered = remembered/been reminded of it
13 cunning, surprising ("too much")
14 come on!
15 naughty, mischievous ("clever for your age")

Archbishop of York	Here comes a messenger. What news?
Messenger	Such news, my lord, as grieves me to unfold.
40 *Elizabeth*	How doth the Prince?
Messenger	Well madam, and in health.
Duchess of York	What is thy news?
Messenger	Lord Rivers and Lord Grey are sent to

Pomfret,[16]

With them Sir Thomas Vaughan, prisoners.

45 *Duchess of York*	Who hath committed them?
Messenger	The mighty dukes, Gloucester and

Buckingham.

Archbishop of York	For what offense?
Messenger	The sum of all I can,[17] I have disclosed.

Why, or for what, the nobles were committed

50 Is all unknown to me, my gracious lord.

Elizabeth Aye me! I see the downfall of my house.

The tiger now hath seized the gentle hind,[18]

Insulting[19] tyranny begins to jut[20]

Upon the innocent and aweless[21] throne.

55 Welcome destruction, blood, and massacre!

I see (as in a map)[22] the end of all.

Duchess of York Accursèd and unquiet[23] wrangling days,

How many of you have mine eyes beheld?

16 Pontefract Castle, scene of many executions
17 know
18 female deer
19 arrogant, scornful, contemptuous
20 encroach
21 unterrifying (i.e., helpless)
22 (1) geographical representation, (2) chart, table
23 disturbed, restless, disordered★

My husband lost his life to get the crown,
And often up and down my sons were tossed,   60
For me to joy, and weep, their gain and loss.
And being seated, and domestic broils[24]
Clean overblown,[25] themselves the conquerors,
Make war upon themselves, brother to brother,
Blood to blood, self against self. O preposterous[26]   65
And frantic outrage, end thy damnèd spleen,[27]
Or let me die, to look on death no more.

Elizabeth   Come, come, my boy, we will to sanctuary.[28]
          Madam, farewell.

Duchess of York   Stay, I will go with you.   70

Elizabeth   You have no cause.

Archbishop of York (to Elizabeth) My gracious lady, go,
          And thither bear your treasure and your goods.
          For my part, I'll resign unto your Grace
          The seal[29] I keep, and so[30] betide to me   75
          As well[31] I tender[32] you and all of yours.
          Come, I'll conduct you to the sanctuary.

EXEUNT

24 turmoils, disturbances, quarrels
25 passed away, blown over
26 perverse, upside down, unnatural (preePAHStrus)
27 (1) whims, caprices, merriment, (2) bad temper, passionate fits, spite, fury★
28 safe house (religious or customary)
29 i.e., the extremely important (and potent) Great Seal of England, entrusted
   to him by Edward IV
30 let whatever
31 while
32 care/have compassion for★

Act 3

SCENE I

London, A street

TRUMPETS SOUND

ENTER YOUNG PRINCE EDWARD, GLOUCESTER,
BUCKINGHAM, CARDINAL, CATESBY, AND OTHERS

Buckingham   Welcome, sweet Prince, to London, to your
  chamber.[1]
Gloucester   Welcome, dear cousin, my thoughts' sovereign.[2]
  The weary way hath made you melancholy.
Prince Edward No uncle, but our crosses[3] on the way
5   Have made it tedious, wearisome, and heavy.
  I want more uncles here to welcome me.
Gloucester   Sweet prince, the untainted[4] virtue of your years
  Hath not yet dived into the world's deceit.
  Nor more can you distinguish of a man

---

1 rooms, apartment ("quarters")
2 lord, master
3 criss-crossing, going one way and then another
4 unblemished ("pure")★

Than of his outward show; which (God he knows)   10
Seldom or never jumpeth[5] with the heart.
Those uncles which you want were dangerous.
Your Grace attended to their sugared words,
But looked not on the poison of their hearts.
God keep you from them, and from such false friends!   15

Prince Edward God keep me from false friends, but they
        were none.

Gloucester   My lord, the Mayor of London comes to
        greet you.

ENTER LORD MAYOR AND ATTENDANTS

Mayor   God bless your Grace with health and happy days.

Prince Edward I thank you, good my lord, and thank you all.
        I thought my mother, and my brother York,   20
        Would long ere this have met us on the way.
        Fie, what a slug[6] is Hastings, that he comes not
        To tell us whether they will come or no!

ENTER HASTINGS

Buckingham   And in good time, here comes the sweating lord.

Prince Edward Welcome, my lord. What, will our mother come?   25

Hastings   On what occasion,[7] God he knows, not I.
        The Queen your mother, and your brother York,
        Have taken sanctuary. The tender[8] Prince
        Would fain have come with me to meet your Grace,

5 coincides
6 slow/lazy fellow
7 on what occasion = when
8 youthful★

30 But by his mother was perforce withheld.

Buckingham Fie, what an indirect[9] and peevish course

Is this of hers! Lord Cardinal, will your Grace

Persuade the Queen to send the Duke of York

Unto his princely brother presently?

35 If she deny,[10] Lord Hastings go with him,

And from her jealous arms pluck him perforce.

Cardinal   My Lord of Buckingham, if my weak oratory

Can from his mother win the Duke of York,

Anon expect him here. But if she be obdurate

40 To mild entreaties, God forbid

We should infringe the holy privilege[11]

Of blessèd sanctuary! Not for all this land

Would I be guilty of so deep a sin.

Buckingham You are too senseless[12] obstinate, my lord,

45 Too ceremonious[13] and traditional.

Weigh[14] it but with the grossness[15] of this age,

You[16] break not sanctuary in seizing him.

The benefit thereof[17] is always granted

To those whose dealings have deserved the place,[18]

50 And those who have the wit to claim the place.

This prince[19] hath neither claimed it, nor deserved it,

9 devious, deceitful
10 refuse★
11 right, advantage★
12 devoid of understanding, foolish, unreasonable
13 given to/bound by formalities
14 consider
15 coarseness, lack of refinement/delicacy
16 and then you will see that
17 of sanctuary
18 the place = sanctuary
19 i.e., the Duke of York is (a) a child and (b) has in any case not himself
   claimed sanctuary

And therefore, in mine opinion, cannot have it.

Then taking him from thence, that is not there,[20]

You break no privilege nor charter[21] there.

Oft have I heard of sanctuary men,   55

But sanctuary children, ne'er till now.

Cardinal   My lord, you shall o'er-rule my mind[22] for once.

Come on, Lord Hastings, will you go with me?

Hastings   I go, my lord.

Prince Edward Good lords, make all the speedy haste you may.   60

EXEUNT CARDINAL AND HASTINGS

Say,[23] uncle Gloucester, if our brother come,

Where shall we sojourn[24] till our coronation?

Gloucester   Where it think'st best unto your royal self.

If I may counsel you, some day or two

Your Highness shall[25] repose you at the Tower.   65

Then[26] where you please, and shall be thought most fit

For your best health and recreation.[27]

Prince Edward I do not like the Tower, of any place.[28]

Did Julius Caesar build that place, my lord?

Buckingham   He did, my gracious lord, begin that place,   70

Which since succeeding ages have re-edified.[29]

20 i.e., that is not in fact someone in sanctuary
21 a document granting privilege
22 thought, purpose, judgment★
23 tell me
24 lodge, take up temporary residence
25 should, ought to
26 afterward
27 comfort
28 any place = all places
29 rebuilt

Prince Edward Is it upon record,[30] or else reported
    Successively[31] from age to age, he built it?
Buckingham   Upon record, my gracious lord.
75 **Prince Edward** But say, my lord, it were not registered,[32]
    Methinks the truth should live from age to age,
    As 'twere retailed[33] to all posterity,
    Even to the general ending day.[34]
Gloucester   (*aside*) So wise so young, they say, do never
    live long.
80 **Prince Edward** What say you, uncle?
Gloucester   I say, without characters,[35] fame lives long.
    (*aside*) Thus, like the formal[36] vice, iniquity,[37]
    I moralize[38] two meanings in one word.
Prince Edward That Julius Caesar was a famous man.
85   With what his valor did enrich his wit,
    His wit set down to make his valor live.
    Death makes no conquest of this conqueror,
    For now he lives in fame, though not in life.
    I'll tell you what, my cousin Buckingham –
90 **Buckingham**   What, my gracious lord?
Prince Edward And if I live until I be a man,
    I'll win our ancient right in France again,

30 written documentation
31 continuously★
32 recounted, recorded, set down★
33 repeated
34 i.e., the Day of Judgment
35 written characters/letters
36 hypocritical
37 Vice and Iniquity are two names for the same character in older morality
    plays
38 interpret, explain

Or die a soldier, as I lived a king.

Gloucester   (*aside*) Short summers lightly have[39] a forward[40]
spring.

ENTER RICHARD (DUKE OF YORK),
HASTINGS, AND CARDINAL

Buckingham   Now, in good time, here comes the Duke of   95
York.

Prince Edward Richard of York, how fares our loving brother?

York   Well, my dear lord — so must I call you now.

Prince Edward Aye, brother, to our grief, as it is yours.
Too late[41] he died that might have kept that title,
Which[42] by his death hath lost much majesty.   100

Gloucester   How fares our cousin, noble Lord of York?

York   I thank you, gentle uncle. O my lord,
You said that idle weeds are fast in growth.
The Prince my brother hath outgrown me far.

Gloucester   He hath, my lord.

York   And therefore is he idle?   105

Gloucester   O my fair cousin, I must not say so.

York   Then he is more beholding to you than I.[43]

Gloucester   He may command me as my sovereign,
But you have power in me, as in a kinsman.

York   I pray you, uncle, give me this dagger.   110

Gloucester   My dagger, little cousin? With all my heart.[44]

39 lightly have = tend to come / stem from
40 precocious, early
41 recently
42 i.e., the title of "king"
43 i.e., your gracious courtesy puts him in your debt
44 i.e., as one can "give" a blow

Prince Edward	A beggar, brother?
York	Of my kind uncle, that I know will give,
	And being[45] but a toy, which is no grief[46] to give.
115 *Gloucester*	A greater gift than that, I'll give my cousin.
York	A greater gift? O, that's the sword to it.
Gloucester	Aye, gentle cousin, were it light enough.
York	O then, I see you will part but with light[47] gifts,
	In weightier things you'll say a beggar nay.
120 *Gloucester*	It is too weighty for your Grace to wear.
York	I weigh[48] it lightly, were it heavier.
Gloucester	What, would you have my weapon, little lord?
York	I would, that[49] I might thank you as you call me.
Gloucester	How?
York	Little.
125 *Prince Edward*	My Lord of York will still[50] be cross[51] in talk.
	Uncle, your Grace knows how to bear with him.
York	You mean, to bear me, not to bear with me.
	Uncle, my brother mocks both you and me.
	Because that I am little, like an ape,[52]
130	He thinks that you should bear me on your shoulders.
Buckingham	*(aside)* With what a sharp, provided[53] wit
	he reasons!
	To mitigate the scorn he gives his uncle,

45 it (the dagger) being
46 hardship, difficulty
47 unimportant
48 value
49 so that
50 will still = always wants to be
51 contrary, perverse
52 monkey
53 prepared, ready★

He prettily and aptly[54] taunts himself.

So cunning, and so young, is wonderful.

Gloucester   (*to Edward*) My lord, will't please you pass   135
along?[55]

Myself and my good cousin Buckingham

Will to your mother, to entreat of her

To meet you at the Tower and welcome you.

York   What, will you go unto[56] the Tower, my lord?

Prince Edward My Lord Protector will have it so.   140

York   I shall not sleep in quiet at the Tower.

Gloucester   Why, what should you fear?

York   Marry, my uncle Clarence's angry ghost.

My grandam told me he was murdered there.

Prince Edward I fear no uncles dead.   145

Gloucester   Nor none that live, I hope.

Prince Edward And if they live, I hope I need not fear.

But come, my lord. And with a heavy heart,

Thinking on them, go I unto the Tower.

A SENNET[57]

EXEUNT ALL BUT GLOUCESTER, BUCKINGHAM,
AND CATESBY

Buckingham   Think you, my lord, this little prating York   150

Was not incensed by his subtle mother

To taunt and scorn you thus opprobriously?[58]

54 appropriately, suitably
55 pass along = proceed on
56 to
57 ceremonial fanfare★
58 abusively

Gloucester   No doubt, no doubt. O 'tis a perilous[59] boy,
　　Bold, quick, ingenious, forward, capable.
155　He is all the mother's, from the top to toe.
Buckingham Well, let them rest. Come hither, Catesby.
　　Thou art sworn as deeply to effect[60] what we intend,
　　As closely to conceal what we impart.[61]
　　Thou know'st our reasons urged upon the way.
160　What think'st thou? Is it not an easy matter
　　To make William Lord Hastings of our mind,
　　For the installment of this noble Duke[62]
　　In the seat royal of this famous isle?
Catesby   He for his father's[63] sake so loves the Prince,
165　That he will not be won to aught against him.
Buckingham What think'st thou then of Stanley? Will not he?
Catesby   He will do all in all as Hastings doth.
Buckingham Well then, no more but this. Go gentle Catesby,
　　And as it were far off[64] sound[65] thou Lord Hastings,
170　How doth he stand affected[66] to our purpose,
　　And summon him tomorrow to the Tower,
　　To sit[67] about the coronation.
　　If thou dost find him tractable[68] to us,
　　Encourage him, and show him all our reasons.

59 dangerous
60 accomplish, bring about★
61 communicate, tell, share
62 Gloucester
63 i.e., the prince's father, Edward IV
64 i.e., in time ("distant")★
65 inquire of★
66 disposed, inclined
67 confer
68 compliant

If he be leaden, icy, cold, unwilling,   175
Be thou so too, and so break off the talk,
And give us notice of his inclination.
For we tomorrow hold divided[69] councils,
Wherein thyself shalt highly be employed.
Gloucester   Commend me to Lord William. Tell him, Catesby,   180
His ancient knot[70] of dangerous adversaries
Tomorrow are[71] let blood at Pomfret Castle,
And bid my friend, for joy of this good news,
Give Mistress Shore one gentle kiss the more.
Buckingham Good Catesby go, effect this business soundly.[72]   185
Catesby   My good lords both, with all the heed[73] I can.
Gloucester   Shall we hear from you, Catesby, ere we sleep?
Catesby   You shall, my lord.
Gloucester   At Crosby House, there shall you find us both.

EXIT CATESBY

Buckingham Now my lord, what shall we do if we perceive   190
Lord Hastings will not yield to our complots?[74]
Gloucester   Chop off his head. Something we will determine.[75]
And look when I am king, claim thou of me
The earldom of Hereford, and the movables[76]
Whereof the King my brother stood possessed.   195

69 i.e., one in public, for show, and one in private, for the real business
70 group, mass
71 are to be
72 (1) thoroughly, (2) covertly
73 attention, care
74 conspiracies
75 put an end to
76 personal property (as opposed to "real property," land)★

Buckingham I'll claim that promise at your Grace's hands.

Gloucester   And look[77] to have it yielded with all willingness.

Come, let us sup betimes,[78] that afterwards

We may digest[79] our complots in some form.

EXEUNT

77 expect
78 early, soon
79 arrange

SCENE 2

In front of Lord Hastings' house

Messenger My lord, my lord!

Hastings (*within*) Who knocks?

Messenger One from the Lord Stanley.

Hastings What is't o'clock?[1]

Messenger   Upon the stroke of four.[2]

Hastings Cannot my Lord Stanley sleep, these tedious nights?   5

Messenger So it appears, by that I have to say.

    First, he commends him to your noble self.

Hastings What then?

Messenger Then certifies[3] your lordship that this night

    He dreamt the boar had razed off[4] his helm.[5]   10

    Besides, he says there are two councils kept,[6]

    And that may be determined at the one

    Which may make you and him to rue[7] at th'other.

    Therefore he sends to know your lordship's pleasure,[8]

    If you will presently take horse with him   15

    And with all speed post with him toward the north,

---

1 what is't o'clock? = what time is it?

2 i.e., 4:00 A.M.

3 declares to

4 razed off = cut off★

5 the boar was Richard of Gloucester's heraldic emblem; the helm ("helmet") here refers to Stanley's head

6 to be held

7 regret

8 your lordship's pleasure = what your lordship wants/likes★

To shun the danger that his soul divines.
Hastings　　Go fellow, go, return unto thy lord,
　　Bid him not fear the separated council.
20　　His honor[9] and myself are at the one,
　　And at the other is my good friend Catesby,
　　Where nothing can proceed that toucheth us
　　Whereof I shall not have intelligence.
　　Tell him his fears are shallow, without instance.[10]
25　　And for[11] his dreams, I wonder he is so simple
　　To trust the mockery of unquiet slumbers.
　　To fly the boar before the boar pursues
　　Were[12] to incense the boar to follow us
　　And make pursuit where he did mean no chase.
30　　Go, bid thy master rise and come to me
　　And we will both together to the Tower,
　　Where he shall see the boar will use[13] us kindly.
Messenger　I'll go, my lord, and tell him what you say.

EXIT MESSENGER

ENTER CATESBY

Catesby　　Many good morrows to my noble lord!
35　*Hastings*　Good morrow, Catesby, you are early stirring.
　　What news, what news, in this our tottering[14] state?
Catesby　　It is a reeling world indeed, my lord,

9 his honor = Stanley himself
10 cause
11 as for
12 would be
13 treat
14 wavering, vacillating

And I believe will never stand upright
Till Richard wear the garland[15] of the realm.

Hastings How wear the garland? Dost thou mean the crown?   40

Catesby Aye, my good lord.

Hastings I'll have this crown[16] of mine cut from my shoulders
Ere I will see the crown so foul misplaced.
But canst thou guess that he doth aim at it?

Catesby Aye, on my life, and hopes to find you forward[17]   45
Upon his party, for the gain thereof.
And thereupon he sends you this good news,
That this same very day your enemies,
The kindred of the Queen, must die at Pomfret.

Hastings Indeed I am no mourner for that news,   50
Because they have been still mine adversaries.
But that I'll give my voice on Richard's side,
To bar my master's heirs in true descent,
God knows I will not do it, to the death.

Catesby God keep your lordship in that gracious mind.   55

Hastings But I shall laugh at this a twelvemonth hence,
That they who brought me in my master's hate
I live to look upon their tragedy.
Well Catesby, ere a fortnight make me older,
I'll send some packing that yet think not on it.   60

Catesby 'Tis a vile thing to die, my gracious lord,
When men are unprepared and look not for it.

Hastings O monstrous, monstrous! And so falls it out
With Rivers, Vaughan, Grey, and so 'twill do

15 wreath ("crown")
16 head
17 eager, ready

65 With some men else, who think themselves as safe
As thou and I, who (as thou know'st) are dear
To princely Richard and to Buckingham.
Catesby The princes both make high account[18] of you,
(*aside*) For they account[19] his head upon the bridge.[20]
70 *Hastings* I know they do, and I have well deserved it.

ENTER STANLEY

Come on, come on, where is your boar spear, man?
Fear you the boar, and go so unprovided?[21]
Stanley My lord, good morrow. Good morrow, Catesby.
You may jest on, but, by the holy rood[22]
75 I do not like these several[23] councils, I.
Hastings My lord, I hold my life as dear as yours,
And never in my days, I do protest,
Was it so precious to me as 'tis now.
Think you, but that I know our state secure,
80 I would be so triumphant[24] as I am?
Stanley The lords at Pomfret, when they rode from London,
Were jocund,[25] and supposed their state was sure,
And they indeed had no cause to mistrust.
But yet you see how soon the day o'ercast.[26]
85 This sudden stab of rancor I misdoubt.[27]

18 reckoning, judgment★
19 calculate, expect
20 i.e., where the heads of traitors were displayed
21 unequipped
22 cross★
23 separate, distinct★
24 exultant★
25 blithe, cheerful★ (JOCKind)
26 darkened ("overcast")
27 have doubts about, mistrust

Pray God, I say, I prove a needless coward!

What, shall we toward the Tower? The day is spent.

Hastings Come, come, have with you. Wot you[28] what,

my lord?

Today the lords you talk of are beheaded.

Stanley They, for their truth,[29] might better wear their heads   90

Than some that have accused them wear their hats.

But come, my lord, let's away.

ENTER A HERALD

Hastings Go on before, I'll talk with this good fellow.

EXEUNT STANLEY AND CATESBY

How now, sirrah?[30] How goes the world with thee?

Herald   The better that your lordship please to ask.   95

Hastings I tell thee man, 'tis better with me now

Than when thou met'st me last where now we meet.

Then was I going prisoner to the Tower,

By the suggestion of the Queen's allies.

But now I tell thee (keep it to thyself)   100

This day those enemies are put to death,

And I in better state than e'er I was.

Herald   God hold it, to your honor's good content!

Hastings Gramercy,[31] fellow. (*throws him his purse*) There, drink

that for me.

Herald   I thank your honor.   105

EXIT HERALD

28 do you know
29 loyalty, fidelity, steadfast allegiance
30 term of address used for people of lower rank than oneself
31 thank you

ENTER A PRIEST

Priest	Well met, my lord, I am glad to see your honor.
Hastings	I thank thee, good Sir John,[32] with all my heart.

I am in your debt for your last exercise.[33]

Come the next Sabbath, and I will content[34] you.

HE WHISPERS IN THE PRIEST'S EAR

ENTER BUCKINGHAM

110 *Priest*   I'll wait upon[35] your lordship.

Buckingham What, talking with a priest, Lord Chamberlain?

Your friends at Pomfret, they do need the priest,

Your honor hath no shriving[36] work in hand.

Hastings   Good faith, and when I met this holy man,

115   Those men you talk of came into my mind.

What, go you toward the Tower?

Buckingham I do, my lord, but long I cannot stay there.

I shall return before your lordship thence.[37]

Hastings   'Tis like enough, for I stay dinner[38] there.

120 *Buckingham* (*aside*) And supper[39] too, although thou know'st
it not.

Come, will you go?

Hastings   I'll wait upon your lordship.

EXEUNT

32 i.e., a man who had taken his first university degree was called "Sir John"
33 declamation, sermon
34 (verb) satisfy, please, gratify (kunTENT)
35 wait upon = await
36 the hearing of confessions
37 from there
38 stay dinner = stay to/for a midday meal
39 last meal of the day

SCENE 3

Pomfret Castle

ENTER RATCLIFF, WITH ARMED MEN, ESCORTING RIVERS,
GREY, AND VAUGHAN TO THEIR EXECUTION

Rivers	Sir Richard Ratcliff, let me tell thee this,
	Today shalt thou behold a subject[1] die
	For truth, for duty, and for loyalty.
Grey	God bless[2] the Prince[3] from all the pack of you!
	A knot you are of damnèd blood-suckers![4]

5

Vaughan	You live, that shall cry woe for this hereafter.
Ratcliff	Dispatch,[5] the limit[6] of your lives is out.
Rivers	O Pomfret, Pomfret! O thou bloody prison,
	Fatal and ominous[7] to noble peers!
	Within the guilty[8] closure[9] of thy walls

10

	Richard the Second here was hacked to death,
	And for more slander[10] to thy dismal seat
	We give thee up our guiltless blood to drink.
Grey	Now Margaret's curse is fall'n upon our heads,
	When she exclaimed on Hastings, you, and I,

15

	For standing by when Richard stabbed her son.
Rivers	Then cursed she Richard, then cursed she
	Buckingham,

1 i.e., someone subject to a ruling king
2 protect, save, guard
3 Richard Duke of York, Prince of Wales
4 a KNOT you ARE of DAMned BLOOD SUCKers
5 hurry up, move along
6 boundary, prescribed time, last stage
7 foreboding evil
8 criminal, guilt-ridden
9 confines
10 discredit, disgrace

Then cursed she Hastings. O remember, God
To hear her prayers for them, as now for us,
20   And for my sister and her princely sons.
Be satisfied, dear God, with our true blood,
Which, as thou know'st, unjustly must be spilt.
Ratcliff Make haste, the hour of death is expiate.[11]
Rivers Come, Grey, come, Vaughan, let us here embrace.
25   Farewell, until we meet again in heaven.

EXEUNT

11 is expatiate = has come/arrived

SCENE 4

The Tower of London

ENTER BUCKINGHAM, STANLEY, HASTINGS, BISHOP OF ELY,
RATCLIFF, LOVEL, WITH OTHERS, AND SIT AT A TABLE

Hastings   Now noble peers, the cause why we are met
  Is to determine of the coronation.
  In God's name, speak, when is the royal day?

Buckingham   Is all things ready for the royal time?

Stanley   It is, and wants but nomination.[1]   5

Bishop of Ely Tomorrow, then, I judge a happy day.

Buckingham   Who knows the Lord Protector's mind herein?
  Who is most inward[2] with the noble Duke?

Bishop of Ely Your Grace, we think, should soonest know
  his mind.

Buckingham   We know each other's faces. For our hearts,   10
  He knows no more of mine than I of yours,
  Or I of his, my lord, than you of mine.
  Lord Hastings, you and he are near in love.

Hastings   I thank his Grace, I know he loves me well.
  But for his purpose in the coronation   15
  I have not sounded him, nor he delivered[3]
  His gracious pleasure any way therein.
  But you, my honorable lords, may name the time,
  And in the Duke's behalf I'll give my voice,
  Which I presume he'll take in gentle part.[4]   20

---

1 action, appointment
2 intimate
3 stated
4 gentle part = noble respect

ENTER GLOUCESTER

Bishop of Ely In happy time, here comes the Duke himself.

Gloucester   My noble lords, and cousins all, good morrow.
  I have been long a sleeper. But I trust
  My absence doth neglect[5] no great design,
25   Which by my presence might have been concluded.

Buckingham   Had not you come upon your cue, my lord,
  William Lord Hastings had pronounced[6] your part –
  I mean, your voice – for crowning of the King.

Gloucester   Than my Lord Hastings no man might be bolder,
30   His lordship knows me well, and loves me well.
  My Lord of Ely, when I was last in Holborne,
  I saw good strawberries in your garden there.
  I do beseech you, send for some of them.

Bishop of Ely Marry, and will, my lord, with all my heart.

EXIT BISHOP

35 *Gloucester*   Cousin of Buckingham, a word with you.
  (*drawing him aside*) Catesby hath sounded Hastings in
  our business,
  And finds the testy[7] gentleman so hot,
  That he will lose his head ere give consent
  His[8] master's child, as worshipfully as he terms it,
40   Shall lose the royalty of England's throne.

Buckingham   Withdraw yourself a while, I'll go with you.

---

5 slight, leave unattended
6 spoken, delivered
7 rash, irascible
8 that his

EXEUNT GLOUCESTER, BUCKINGHAM FOLLOWING

Stanley   We have not yet set down this day of triumph.
   Tomorrow, in my judgment, is too sudden,
   For I myself am not so well provided
   As else I would be, were the day prolonged.⁹   45

ENTER BISHOP OF ELY

Bishop of Ely Where is my lord, the Duke of Gloucester?
   I have sent for these strawberries.
Hastings   His Grace looks cheerfully and smooth this
   morning,
   There's some conceit or other likes him well,
   When he doth bid good morrow with such a spirit.   50
   I think there's never a man in Christendom
   Can lesser hide his love, or hate, than he,
   For by his face straight shall you know his heart.
Stanley   What of his heart perceive you in his face
   By any likelihood¹⁰ he showed today?   55
Hastings   Marry, that with no man here he is offended.
   For were he, he had shown it in his looks.
Stanley   I pray God he be not, I say.

ENTER GLOUCESTER AND BUCKINGHAM

Gloucester   I pray you all, tell me what they deserve
   That do conspire my death with devilish plots   60
   Of damnèd witchcraft, and that have prevailed
   Upon my body with their hellish charms?

9 lengthened, extended
10 sign, probability

Hastings   The tender love I bear your Grace, my lord,
            Makes me most forward in this noble presence
65   To doom th'offenders, whosoever they be.
            I say, my lord, they have deservèd death.
Gloucester Then be your eyes the witness of their evil.
            Look how I am bewitched. Behold, mine arm
            Is like a blasted[11] sapling, withered up.
70   And this[12] is Edward's wife, that monstrous witch,
            Consorted[13] with that harlot strumpet Shore,
            That by their witchcraft thus have marked me.
Hastings   If they have done this thing, my noble lord –
Gloucester If? Thou protector of this damnèd strumpet,
75   Talkst thou to me of "ifs"? Thou art a traitor,
            Off with his head! Now by Saint Paul I swear,
            I will not dine until I see the same.
            Lovel and Ratcliff, look that it be done.
            The rest that love me, rise, and follow me.

         EXEUNT ALL BUT HASTINGS, RATCLIFF, AND LOVEL

80 *Hastings*   Woe, woe for England, not a whit[14] for me,
            For I, too fond,[15] might have prevented this.
            Stanley did dream the boar did raze our helms,
            And I did scorn it, and disdain[16] to fly.
            Three times today my foot-cloth[17] horse did stumble,

---

11 blighted, lightning-struck
12 it
13 joined★
14 bit (the smallest amount)
15 foolish★
16 scorn★
17 gentlemen's horses sometimes wore a long, elaborately ornamented cloth
   across their backs, hanging down on both sides

And started when he looked upon the Tower,   85
As[18] loath to bear me to the slaughterhouse.
O now I need the priest that spake to me.
I now repent I told the pursuivant,[19]
As too triumphing, how mine enemies
Today at Pomfret bloodily were butchered,   90
And I myself secure in grace and favor.
O Margaret, Margaret, now thy heavy curse
Is lighted on poor Hastings' wretched head!

Ratcliff   Come, come, dispatch, the Duke would[20] be at dinner.
Make a short shrift,[21] he longs to see your head.   95

Hastings   O momentary grace of mortal men,
Which we more hunt for than the grace of God!
Who[22] builds his hopes in air[23] of your good looks,
Lives like a drunken sailor on a mast,
Ready with every nod to tumble down   100
Into the fatal bowels of the deep.

Lovel   Come, come, dispatch, 'tis bootless[24] to exclaim.

Hastings   O bloody Richard! Miserable England,
I prophesy the fearful'st time to thee
That ever wretched age hath looked upon.   105
Come, lead me to the block, bear him my head.
They smile at me, who shortly shall be dead.

EXEUNT

18 as if
19 herald★
20 wishes to
21 confession
22 he who
23 in air = in castles in the air ("of airy")
24 useless, hopeless

SCENE 5

The Tower walls

ENTER GLOUCESTER AND BUCKINGHAM,
WEARING RUSTED, UGLY ARMOR

Gloucester   Come cousin, canst thou quake, and change
　　thy color,
　　Murder[1] thy breath in middle of a word,
　　And then begin again, and stop again,
　　As if thou wert distraught and mad with terror?

5 *Buckingham* Tut, I can counterfeit the deep[2] tragedian,
　　Speak, and look back, and pry[3] on every side,
　　Tremble and start at wagging of a straw,
　　Intending[4] deep suspicion. Ghastly looks
　　Are at my service, like enforcèd smiles,

10　And both are ready in their offices[5]
　　At any time to grace my stratagems.
　　But what, is Catesby gone?

Gloucester   He is, and see, he brings the Mayor[6] along.

ENTER LORD MAYOR AND CATESBY

Buckingham Lord Mayor —

15 *Gloucester*   Look to[7] the drawbridge[8] there!

1 butcher, lose control of, cut off
2 great, profound, solemn
3 peer, look
4 signifying★
5 services, duties, responsibilities★
6 Lord Mayor of London
7 look to = take care of/attend to
8 i.e., the Tower was a military installation – walled, with a moat and
　　drawbridge

Buckingham	Hark! A drum.
Gloucester	Catesby, o'erlook[9] the walls.
Buckingham	Lord Mayor, the reason we have sent –
Gloucester	Look back, defend thee, here are[10] enemies.
Buckingham	God and our innocency defend and guard us!

20

Gloucester   Be patient,[11] they are friends – Ratcliff and Lovel.

ENTER LOVEL AND RATCLIFF, WITH HASTINGS' HEAD

Lovel   Here is the head of that ignoble[12] traitor,
The dangerous and unsuspected Hastings.

Gloucester   So dear I loved the man, that I must weep.
I took him for the plainest harmless creature   25
That breathed upon this earth, a Christian,
Made him my book wherein my soul recorded
The history of all her secret thoughts.
So smooth he daubed[13] his vice with show of virtue
That, his apparent[14] open guilt omitted –   30
I mean, his conversation[15] with Shore's wife –
He lived from all attainder of suspect.[16]

Buckingham   Well, well, he was the covert'st[17] sheltered traitor
That ever lived.
Would you imagine, or almost[18] believe –   35

---

9 superintend, inspect, take car of
10 come
11 composed (military usage, "at ease")
12 dishonorable, base
13 covered, coated
14 plain, visible
15 intimacy, sexual intercourse
16 attainder of suspects = accusation of suspicions
17 most hidden
18 ever

Were't not that, by great preservation,[19]
We live to tell it you – the subtle traitor
This day had plotted, in the council-house
To murder me and my good Lord of Gloucester?

40 *Lord Mayor* Had he done so?

Gloucester   What? Think you we are Turks, or infidels?
Or that we would, against the form[20] of law,
Proceed thus rashly to the villain's death,
But that the extreme peril of the case,

45 The peace of England and our persons' safety,
Enforced us to this execution?

Lord Mayor Now fair befall you, he deserved his death,
And your good Graces both have well proceeded,
To warn[21] false traitors from the like attempts.

50 *Buckingham* I never looked for better at his hands,
After he once fell in[22] with Mistress Shore.
Yet had not we determined he should die
Until your lordship came to see his end,
Which now the loving haste of these our friends,

55 Something against our meanings, have prevented.[23]
Because, my lord, I would have had you heard
The traitor speak, and timorously[24] confess
The manner and the purpose of his treasons,
That you might well have signified the same

60 Unto the citizens, who haply may

19 divine intervention (were't NOT that BY great PREserVAseeOWN)
20 good order, rule
21 (1) prevent, (2) caution
22 fell in = taken up with
23 outstripped, anticipated, gone beyond
24 fearfully★

Misconster[25] us in him, and wail his death.

Lord Mayor   But, my good lord, your Grace's word shall serve

As well as I had seen and heard him speak.

And do not doubt you not, right noble princes both,

But I'll acquaint our duteous citizens   65

With all your just proceedings in this cause.

Gloucester   And to that end we wished your lordship here,

T'avoid the censures of the carping[26] world.

Buckingham   Which since you come too late of our intent,

Yet witness what you hear we did intend.   70

And so, my good lord Mayor, we bid farewell.

EXIT LORD MAYOR

Gloucester   Go after, after, cousin Buckingham.

The mayor toward Guildhall[27] hies him in all post.

There, at your meetest advantage[28] of the time,

Infer[29] the bastardy of Edward's children.   75

Tell them how Edward put to death a citizen,

Only for saying he would make his son

Heir to the crown, meaning indeed his house,[30]

Which by the sign thereof was termèd so.

Moreover, urge his hateful luxury[31]   80

And bestial appetite in change[32] of lust,

25 misconstrue
26 chattering, fault-finding
27 London's town hall
28 circumstance, position★
29 introduce, allege★
30 inn-house, tavern
31 lasciviousness
32 changing, succession ("exchanging")

Which stretched unto their servants, daughters, wives,

Even where his lustful eye or savage heart,

Without control, lusted to make a prey.

85 Nay, for a need, thus far come near my person.

Tell them when that my mother went with child

Of that insatiate[33] Edward, noble York,

My princely father, then had wars in France

And by true computation of the time

90 Found that the issue was not his begot,[34]

Which well appearèd in his lineaments,[35]

Being nothing like the noble Duke my father.

But touch this sparingly, as 'twere far off,

Because, my lord, you know my mother lives.

95 *Buckingham* Fear not, my lord, I'll play the orator

As if the golden fee[36] for which I plead

Were for myself. And so, my lord, adieu.

Gloucester   If you thrive well, bring them to Baynard's Castle,[37]

Where you shall find me well accompanied

100 With reverend fathers and well-learnèd bishops.

Buckingham I go, and toward three or four o'clock[38]

Look for the news that the Guildhall affordeth.[39]

EXIT BUCKINGHAM

Gloucester   Go Lovel with all speed to Doctor[40] Shaw.

33 insatiable, never satisfied
34 (verb) procreated, generated
35 features (LINaMENTS)★
36 estate, inheritance, lordship
37 located on the Thames River
38 i GO and TOWards THREE or FOUR oCLOCK
39 look FOR the NEWS that THE guildHALL afFORdeth (?)
40 i.e., Reverend Doctor

(*to Catesby? Ratcliff?*) Go thou to Friar Penker. Bid them both
Meet me within this hour at Baynard's Castle.   105

EXEUNT ALL BUT GLOUCESTER

Now will I in, to take[41] some privy[42] order
To draw[43] the brats of Clarence out of sight,
And to give notice that no manner[44] person
Have any[45] time recourse[46] unto the princes.

EXIT

41 make★
42 secret
43 remove
44 no manner = absolutely no
45 at any
46 access

SCENE 6

A street

ENTER A SCRIVENER,[1] WITH A DOCUMENT IN HIS HAND

Scrivener This is the indictment[2] of the good Lord Hastings
Which in a set[3] hand fairly is engrossed,[4]
That it may be today read over[5] in Paul's.
And mark how well the sequel[6] hangs together.
5 Eleven hours I have spent to write it over,
For yesternight by Catesby was it sent me.
The precedent[7] was full as long a-doing,
And yet within these five hours Hastings lived,
Untainted, unexamined,[8] free, at liberty.
10 Here's a good world the while! Who is so gross[9]
That seeth not this palpable device?[10]
Yet who so bold but says he sees it not?
Bad is the world, and all will come to nought,
When such bad dealings must be seen in thought.[11]

EXIT

1 professional copyist/preparer of documents
2 formal accusation
3 ceremonial, formal, elaborate
4 fairly is engrossed = is handsomely/beautifully/elegantly written in large letters
5 fully, completely
6 sequence, sequential ordering (that which follows)★
7 original draft
8 not yet interrogated (sometimes under torture)
9 dense, thick-headed, stupid
10 palpable invention = obvious/patent invention/scheme/contrivance
11 in thought = only in thought ("silently")

SCENE 7

Baynard's Castle

ENTER GLOUCESTER AND BUCKINGHAM,
AT DIFFERENT DOORS

Gloucester	How now, how now, what say the citizens?
Buckingham	Now by the holy Mother of our Lord,

    The citizens are mum, say not a word.

Gloucester	Touched you the bastardy of Edward's children?
Buckingham	I did, with his contract with Lady Lucy,[1] 5

    And his contract by deputy in France,[2]

    The insatiate greediness of his desires,

    And his enforcement of[3] the city wives,

    His tyranny for[4] trifles, his own bastardy,

    As being got, your father then in France,   10

    His resemblance being not like the Duke.

    Withal, I did infer your lineaments

    Being the right idea[5] of your father,

    Both in your form and nobleness of mind –

    Laid[6] open all your victories in Scotland,   15

    Your discipline in war, wisdom in peace,

    Your bounty,[7] virtue, fair humility –

    Indeed, left nothing fitting for the purpose

---

1 Elizabeth Lucy, to whom Edward was alleged (but never proved) to have been engaged to marry
2 i.e., Warwick, as Edward's emissary, went to Paris to arrange a marriage
3 enforcement of = forcing
4 on account/because of
5 right idea = exact/correct image/picture
6 I laid
7 (1) worth, excellence, (2) kindness, generosity

Untouched, or slightly[8] handled, in discourse.

20 And when mine oratory grew to an end
I bid them that did love their country's good
Cry, "God save Richard, England's royal king!"

Gloucester And did they so?

Buckingham No, so God help me, they spake not a word,

25 But like dumb statues, or breathing stones,
Stared each on other, and looked deadly pale.
Which when I saw, I reprehended[9] them,
And asked the Mayor what meant this willful silence?
His answer was, the people were not wont

30 To be spoke to but by the Recorder.[10]
Then he was urged to tell my tale again.
"Thus saith the Duke, thus hath the Duke inferred,"
But nothing spoke in warrant[11] from himself.
When he had done, some followers of mine own,

35 At the lower end of the hall, hurled up their caps,
And some ten voices cried, "God save King Richard!"
And thus I took the vantage of those few,
"Thanks gentle citizens, and friends," quoth I,
"This general applause, and cheerful shower,[12]

40 Argues[13] your wisdoms and your love to Richard."
And even here brake off, and came away.

Gloucester What tongueless blocks were they!
Would not they speak?

8 lightly, casually
9 criticized, scolded
10 magistrate
11 pledge
12 copious outburst
13 indicates★

Buckingham	No, by my troth, my lord.
Gloucester	Will not the Mayor then, and his brethren, come?

Buckingham The Mayor is here at hand. Intend[14] some fear,   45
   Be not you spoke with but[15] by mighty suit.
   And look you get a prayerbook in your hand,
   And stand betwixt two churchmen, good my lord,
   For on that ground I'll build a holy descant.[16]
   And be not easily won to our requests,   50
   Play the maid's part, still[17] answer nay, and take[18] it.

Gloucester I go. And if you plead as well for them
   As I can say nay to thee for myself,
   No doubt we bring it to a happy issue.

Buckingham Go, go, up to the leads,[19] the Lord Mayor knocks.   55

EXIT GLOUCESTER

ENTER THE LORD MAYOR AND CITIZENS

   Welcome my lord, I dance attendance[20] here,
   I think the Duke will not be spoke withal.[21]

ENTER CATESBY

   Now Catesby, what says your lord to my request?

Catesby He doth entreat your Grace, my noble lord,
   To visit him tomorrow, or next day.   60

---

14 indicate, show
15 spoke with but = spoken to except by
16 ground (in music) = foundation, bass-line; descant = melody
17 always
18 then accept
19 lead strips on the roof
20 dance attendance = hang about, ready and waiting
21 with

He is within, with two right reverend fathers,
Divinely bent to meditation,[22]
And no worldly suit would[23] he be moved
To draw him from his holy exercise.[24]

65 *Buckingham* Return, good Catesby, to the gracious Duke,
Tell him, myself, the Mayor and Aldermen,
In deep designs and matters of great moment,
No less importing[25] than our general good,
Are come to have some conference with his Grace.

70 *Catesby* I'll signify so much to him straight.

EXIT CATESBY

Buckingham Ah ha, my lord, this prince is not an Edward,
He is not lolling[26] on a lewd love-bed,
But on his knees, at meditation –
Not dallying with a brace of courtesans,[27]
75 But meditating with two deep divines –
Not sleeping, to engross[28] his idle body,
But praying, to enrich his watchful soul.
Happy were England, would this gracious prince
Take on himself the sovereignty thereof.
80 But sure I fear we shall not win him to it.
Lord Mayor Marry, God defend his Grace should say us nay.
Buckingham I fear he will. Here Catesby comes again.

22 devotion, prayer (MEdiTAYseeOWN)
23 wishes
24 employment, activity
25 involving
26 reclining, resting
27 brace of courtesans = pair of prostitutes
28 fatten up

Now Catesby, what says his Grace?

Catesby   He wonders to what end you have assembled

Such troops of citizens, to come with him,   85

His Grace not being warned thereof before.

He fears, my lord, you mean no good to him.

Buckingham Sorry I am my noble cousin should

Suspect me, that I mean no good to him.

By heaven, we come to him in perfect love.   90

And so once more return and tell his Grace.

EXIT CATESBY

When holy and devout religious men

Are at their beads,[29] 'tis much to draw them thence,

So sweet is zealous[30] contemplation.[31]

ENTER GLOUCESTER ALOFT, BETWEEN TWO BISHOPS

CATESBY RETURNS

Lord Mayor See where his Grace stands, between two   95
clergymen.

Buckingham Two props of virtue for a Christian prince,

To stay him from the fall of vanity.

And see, a book of prayer in his hand,

True ornaments[32] to know a holy man.

(*to Gloucester*) Famous Plantagenet, most gracious prince,   100

---

29 prayers, devotions
30 ardent, enthusiastic
31 CONtemPLAYseeOWN
32 accessories, embellishments

Lend favorable ear to our requests,
And pardon us the interruption
Of thy devotion and right Christian zeal.

Gloucester   My lord, there needs no such apology.

105   I do beseech your Grace to pardon me,
Who, earnest in the service of my God,
Deferred[33] the visitation of my friends.
But leaving this, what is your Grace's pleasure?

Buckingham Even that, I hope, which pleaseth God above,

110   And all good men of this ungoverned isle.

Gloucester   I do suspect I have done some offense
That seems disgracious[34] in the city's eyes,
And that you come to reprehend my ignorance.

Buckingham You have, my lord. Would it might please
your Grace,

115   On our entreaties, to amend your fault.

Gloucester   Else wherefore breathe I in a Christian land?

Buckingham Know then, it is your fault that you resign
The supreme seat, the throne majestical,
The sceptered[35] office of your ancestors,

120   Your state of fortune, and your due[36] of birth,
The lineal glory of your royal house,
To the corruption of a blemished stock.[37]
Whiles in the mildness of your sleepy thoughts,
Which here we waken to our country's good,

33 set aside, put off
34 disliked, disgraceful
35 regal, kingly
36 right, debt★
37 to the corruption of a blemished stock = thus contributing to the
dissolution / destruction of a defective / stained race

The noble isle doth want his proper limbs,   125
His face defaced with scars of infamy,
His royal stock graft[38] with ignoble plants,
And almost shouldered in[39] the swallowing gulf
Of dark forgetfulness and deep oblivion.
Which to recure,[40] we heartily solicit   130
Your gracious self to take on you the charge
And kingly government of this your land,
Not as Protector, steward, substitute,
Or lowly factor[41] for another's gain,
But as successively from blood to blood,   135
Your right of birth, your empery,[42] your own.
For this, consorted with the citizens,
Your very worshipful and loving friends,
And by their vehement instigation,
In this just suit come I to move your Grace.   140
Gloucester I know not whether to depart in silence,
Or bitterly to speak in your reproof[43]
Best fitteth my degree or your condition.
If not to answer, you might haply think
Tongue-tied ambition, not replying, yielded   145
To bear the golden yoke of sovereignty,
Which fondly you would here impose on me.
If to reprove you for this suit of yours,

38 joined ("interbed")
39 shouldered in = thrust into
40 cure, restore
41 agent
42 status, dignity
43 reproach

So seasoned[44] with your faithful love to me.
150 Then on the other side I checked my friends.
Therefore to speak, and to avoid the first,
And then in speaking not to incur the last,
Definitively thus I answer you.
Your love deserves my thanks, but my desert
155 Unmeritable[45] shuns[46] your high request.
First, if all obstacles were cut away,
And that my path were even to the crown,
As the ripe revenue and due of birth,
Yet so much is my poverty of spirit,
160 So mighty and so many my defects,
That I would rather hide me from my greatness,
Being a bark[47] to brook no mighty sea,
Than in my greatness covet[48] to be hid,
And in the vapor[49] of my glory smothered.
165 But God be thanked, there's no need of me,
And much I need,[50] to help you, were there need.
The royal tree hath left us royal fruit,
Which mellowed by the stealing[51] hours of time
Will well become the seat of majesty,
170 And make (no doubt) us happy by his reign.
On him I lay that[52] you would lay on me,

44 mixed, spiced
45 undeserved
46 flees from, avoids
47 small boat★
48 desire
49 steam and other such cloudy/misty emanations
50 much I need = a great deal I lack and would require
51 creeping
52 that which

The right and fortune of his happy stars,
Which God defend that I should wring[53] from him.
Buckingham My lord, this argues conscience in your Grace,
But the respects thereof are nice,[54] and trivial,   175
All circumstances well considered.
You say that Edward is your brother's son.
So say we too, but not by Edward's wife,
For first he was contract[55] to Lady Lucy –
Your mother lives a witness to his vow –   180
And afterward by substitute[56] betrothed
To Bona, sister to the King of France.
These both put off, a poor petitioner,[57]
A care-crazed mother to a many sons,
A beauty-waning and distressèd widow,   185
Even in the afternoon of her best days,
Made prize and purchase[58] of his wanton eye,
Seduced the pitch and height[59] of his degree
To base declension[60] and loathèd bigamy.
By her, in his unlawful bed, he got   190
This Edward, whom our manners[61] term the Prince.
More bitterly could I expostulate,
Save that, for reverence to some alive,
I give a sparing limit to my tongue.

53 squeeze out
54 overly fastidious, fussy
55 (verb) conTRACT
56 proxy
57 i.e., she was the aggressor and actively pursued Edward IV
58 prize and purchase = capture and robbery
59 pitch and height = towering height
60 sinking, declining
61 customs, procedures

195 Then good my lord, take to your royal self
This proffered benefit of dignity,
If not to bless us and the land withal,
Yet to draw forth[62] your noble ancestry
From the corruption of abusing times,
200 Unto a lineal true-derivèd course.

Lord Mayor Do, good my lord, your citizens entreat you.
Buckingham Refuse not, mighty lord, this proffered love.
Catesby O make them joyful, grant their lawful suit!
Gloucester Alas, why would you heap this care on me?
205 I am unfit for state and majesty.
I do beseech you take it not amiss.
I cannot nor I will not yield to you.

Buckingham If you refuse it — as in love and zeal,
Loath to depose the child, your brother's son
210 (As well we know your tenderness of heart
And gentle, kind, effeminate remorse,
Which we have noted in you to your kin,
And egally[63] indeed to all estates) —
Yet whether you accept our suit, or no,
215 Your brother's son shall never reign our king,
But we will plant[64] some other in the throne,
To the disgrace and downfall of your house.
And in this resolution[65] here we leave you.
Come citizens, we will entreat no more.

EXEUNT BUCKINGHAM AND CITIZENS

62 draw forth = remove
63 equally
64 place
65 decision

Catesby	Call him again, sweet prince, accept their suit.	220

    If you deny them, all the land will rue it.

Gloucester   Would you enforce me to a world of care?

    Call them again, I am not made of stones,

    But penetrable to your kind entreaties,

    Albeit[66] against my conscience and my soul.   225

ENTER BUCKINGHAM AND CITIZENS

    Cousin of Buckingham, and sage, grave[67] men,

    Since you will buckle fortune on my back,

    To bear her burthen, whether I will or no,

    I must have patience to endure the load.

    But if black scandal or foul-faced reproach   230

    Attend the sequel of your imposition,[68]

    Your mere[69] enforcement shall acquittance[70] me

    From all the impure blots and stains thereof,

    For God doth know, and you may partly[71] see,

    How far I am from the desire of this.   235

Lord Mayor   God bless your Grace, we see it, and will say it.

Gloucester   In saying so, you shall but say the truth.

Buckingham   Then I salute you with this royal title:

    Long live King Richard, England's worthy king!

Lord Mayor and Citizens   Amen.   240

Buckingham   Tomorrow may it please you to

    be crowned?

---

66 even though (allBEEit)
67 sage, grave = wise/judicious, influential/respected/weighty
68 laying on, imposing
69 absolute
70 (verb) discharge
71 to some degree★

Gloucester   Even when you please, since you will have it so.

Buckingham Tomorrow then we will attend your Grace,

  And so most joyfully we take our leave.

245 Gloucester   (*to the Bishops*) Come, let us to our holy work again.

  Farewell my cousins, farewell gentle friends.

EXEUNT

Act 4

SCENE I

Before the Tower

ENTER, ON ONE SIDE, QUEEN ELIZABETH,
THE DUCHESS OF YORK, AND DORSET, AND ON
THE OTHER, LADY ANNE, LEADING LADY MARGARET
AND CLARENCE'S YOUNG DAUGHTER

Duchess of York Who meets us here? My niece Plantagenet
   Led in the hand of her kind aunt of Gloucester?[1]
   Now, for my life, she's wandr'ing[2] to the Tower,
   On[3] pure heart's love, to greet the tender Princes.
   Daughter, well met.

Anne   God give your Graces both   5
   A happy and a joyful time of day.

Elizabeth   As much to you, good sister. Whither away?

Anne   No farther than the Tower, and as I guess
   Upon the like devotion as yourselves,

1 i.e., Lady Anne, now married to the Duke of Gloucester
2 strolling
3 out of

10   To gratulate⁴ the gentle Princes there.
    Elizabeth   Kind sister, thanks; we'll enter all together.

ENTER BRAKENBURY

    And in good time, here the Lieutenant comes.
    Master Lieutenant, pray you, by your leave,
    How doth the Prince, and my young son of York?
15   *Brakenbury*   Right well, dear madam. By your patience,
    I may not suffer you to visit them.
    The King hath straitly charged the contrary.
    Elizabeth   The King? Who's that?
    Brakenbury   I mean the Lord
    Protector.
    Elizabeth   The Lord protect⁵ him from that kingly title!
20   Hath he set bounds⁶ betwixt their love and me?
    I am their mother, who shall bar me from them?
    Duchess of York I am their father's mother, I will⁷ see them.
    Anne   Their aunt I am in law, in love their mother.
    Then bring me to their sights, I'll bear thy blame
25   And take thy office from thee, on my peril.
    Brakenbury   No, madam, no, I may not leave it so.
    I am bound by oath, and therefore pardon me.

EXIT BRAKENBURY

ENTER STANLEY

    Stanley   Let me but meet you ladies one hour hence,
    And I'll salute your Grace of York as mother

4 greet, welcome
5 defend, preserve
6 boundary lines, limits
7 (1) wish to, (2) am going to

And reverend looker-on[8] of two fair queens.   30
(*to Anne*) Come madam, you must straight to Westminster,
There to be crownèd Richard's royal queen.

Elizabeth Ah, cut my lace[9] asunder,
That my pent[10] heart may have some scope[11] to beat,
Or else I swoon with this dead-killing news!   35

Anne   Despiteful[12] tidings, O unpleasing news!

Dorset   Be of good cheer. (*to Elizabeth*) Mother, how fares
your Grace?

Elizabeth O Dorset, speak not to me, get thee gone,
Death and destruction dog thee at thy heels,
Thy mother's name is ominous[13] to children.   40
If thou wilt outstrip death, go cross the seas,
And live with Richmond,[14] from[15] the reach of hell
Go hie thee, hie thee from this slaughterhouse,
Lest thou increase the number of the dead
And make me die the thrall[16] of Margaret's curse,   45
Nor[17] mother, wife, nor England's counted[18] queen.

Stanley   Full of wise care is this your counsel, madam.
(*to Dorset*) Take all the swift advantage of the hours.
You shall have letters from me to my son[19]

---

8 looker-on = beholder, witness, spectator
9 the string/cord tying her bodice
10 confined
11 room, reach*
12 malignant, spiteful
13 foreboding evil, inauspicious, dangerous
14 the future Henry VII, now and for many years in France
15 away from, out of
16 captive, slave
17 neither
18 acknowledged
19 i.e., Richmond, who is his wife's son

50   In your behalf, to meet you on the way.
      Be not ta'en[20] tardy by unwise delay.
      Duchess of York O ill-dispersing[21] wind of misery,
      O my accursèd womb, the bed of death!
      A cockatrice[22] hast thou hatched to the world,
55   Whose unavoided eye is murderous.
      Stanley   (*to Anne*) Come, madam, come, I in all haste
      was sent.
      Anne   And I with all unwillingness will go.
      I would to God that the inclusive verge[23]
      Of golden metal that must round my brow
60   Were red-hot steel, to sear me to the brains.
      Anointed[24] let me be with deadly venom,
      And die ere men can say, God save the Queen!
      Elizabeth   Go, go, poor soul, I envy not thy glory.
      To feed my humor, wish thyself no harm.
65   *Anne*   No. Why? When he that is my husband now
      Came to me, as I followed Henry's corse,
      When scarce the blood was well washed from his hands
      Which issued from my other angel husband,
      And that dead saint which then I weeping followed –
70   O when, I say, I looked on Richard's face,
      This was my wish: "Be thou," quoth I, "accursed
      For making me, so young, so old a widow!
      And when thou wed'st, let sorrow haunt thy bed,

20 caught★
21 evil-spreading
22 basilisk
23 inclusive verge = enclosing rim
24 rubbed, besmeared

And be thy wife, if any be so mad,

More miserable[25] by the life of thee   75

Than thou hast made me by my dear lord's death!"

Lo, ere I can repeat this curse again,

Even in so short a space,[26] my woman's heart

Grossly grew captive to his honey words

And proved the subject of my own soul's curse,   80

Which ever since hath kept my eyes from rest.

For never yet one hour in his bed

Have I enjoyed the golden dew of sleep,

But with his timorous dreams was still[27] awaked.

Besides, he hates me for my father Warwick,   85

And will (no doubt) shortly be rid of me.

Elizabeth	Poor heart adieu, I pity thy complaining.[28]
Anne	No more than from my soul I mourn for yours.
Elizabeth	Farewell, thou woeful welcomer of glory.
Anne	Adieu, poor soul, that tak'st thy leave of it.

Duchess of York (*to Dorset*) Go thou to Richmond, and good

fortune guide thee.

(*to Anne*) Go thou to Richard, and good angels guard thee.

(*to Elizabeth*) Go thou to sanctuary, and good thoughts

possess thee.

I to my grave, where peace and rest lie with me.

Eighty odd years of sorrow have I seen,   95

And each hour's joy wracked with a week of teen.[29]

25 MIzeRAble
26 time
27 always
28 expression of sorrow/lament
29 trouble, woe

Elizabeth Stay, yet look back with me unto the Tower.
  Pity, you ancient stones, those tender babes
  Whom envy hath immured within your walls,
100 Rough cradle for such little pretty ones.
  Rude ragged nurse, old sullen playfellow
  For tender princes, use my babies well.
  So foolish sorrow bids your stones farewell.

EXEUNT

SCENE 2

London, The palace

SENNET. ENTER KING RICHARD III, IN POMP, CROWNED,
BUCKINGHAM, CATESBY, A PAGE, AND OTHERS

Richard[1]	Stand all apart![2] Cousin of Buckingham.
Buckingham	My gracious sovereign.
Richard	Give me thy hand.

RICHARD ASCENDS HIS THRONE

TRUMPETS

	Thus high, by thy advice,	
And thy assistance, is King Richard seated.		
But shall we wear these honors for[3] a day?		5
Or shall they last, and we rejoice in them?		
Buckingham	Still[4] live they and for ever may they last.	
Richard	Ah Buckingham, now do I play the touch,[5]	
To try if thou be current gold indeed		
Young Edward lives, think now what I would speak.		10
Buckingham	Say on, my loving lord.	
Richard	Why Buckingham, I say I would be king.	
Buckingham	Why so you are, my thrice renownèd liege.[6]	
Richard	Ha? Am I king? 'Tis so. But Edward lives.	
Buckingham	True, noble prince.	

1 until now titled Gloucester
2 to the side
3 for only
4 always, forever
5 play the touch = exercise/bring into action the examination
6 lord★

15   *Richard*   O bitter consequence,[7]

      That Edward still should live[8] true noble prince!

      Cousin, thou wast not wont to be so dull.

      Shall I be plain? I wish the bastards[9] dead,

      And I would have it suddenly performed.

20   What say'st thou? Speak suddenly; be brief.

  Buckingham Your Grace may do your pleasure.

  Richard   Tut, tut, thou art all ice, thy kindness freezeth.

      Say, have I thy consent[10] that they shall[11] die?

  Buckingham Give me some little breath, some pause, dear lord

25   Before I positively[12] speak in this.

      I will resolve[13] you herein presently.

EXIT BUCKINGHAM

  Catesby   (*aside*) The King is angry, see, he gnaws his lip.

  Richard   (*aside*) I will converse[14] with iron-witted[15] fools

      And unrespective[16] boys. None are for me

30   That look into me with considerate[17] eyes.

      High-reaching Buckingham grows circumspect.[18]

      Boy!

  Page   My lord?

7 sequence★
8 live and be a
9 i.e., the illegitimate children
10 agreement
11 must/will
12 explicitly, directly
13 answer, explain, solve for★
14 consort, live/keep company with
15 stupid, dull
16 undiscriminating, heedless
17 thoughtful, deliberate, prudent
18 cautious

Richard Know'st thou not any, whom corrupting gold
   Will tempt unto a close exploit[19] of death?   35
Page   I know a discontented gentleman,
   Whose humble means match[20] not his haughty spirit.
   Gold were as good as twenty orators,
   And will (no doubt) tempt him to any thing.
Richard What is his name?
Page   His name, my lord, is <u>Tyrrel.</u>   40
Richard I partly know the man. Go, call him hither,
   Boy.

EXIT PAGE

   The deep-revolving[21] witty Buckingham
   No more shall be the neighbor to my counsels.
   Hath he so long held out with me, untired,   45
   And stops he now for breath? Well, be it so.

ENTER STANLEY

   How now, Lord Stanley, what's the news?
Stanley Know, my loving lord, the Marquis Dorset
   As I hear is fled to Richmond,
   In those parts where he abides.[22]   50
Richard Come hither Catesby. Rumor it abroad
   That Anne my wife is <u>very grievous sick.</u>
   I will take order for her keeping close.
   Inquire me out some mean[23] poor gentleman,

19 feat, deed
20 equal★
21 turning over in the mind
22 dwells★
23 of middling status / rank

55 Whom I will marry straight to Clarence' daughter.
    The boy[24] is foolish, and I fear not him.
    Look how thou dream'st![25] I say again, give out
    That Anne my queen is sick and like to die.
    About it,[26] for it stands me much upon,[27]
60 To stop all hopes whose growth may damage me.

EXIT CATESBY

    I must be married to my brother's daughter,
    Or else my kingdom stands on brittle glass.
    Murder her brothers, and then marry her —
    Uncertain way of gain. But I am in
65 So far in blood that sin will pluck on sin.
    Tear-falling pity dwells not in this eye.

ENTER PAGE, WITH TYRREL

    Is thy name Tyrrel?
    Tyrrel James Tyrrel, and your most obedient subject.
    Richard Art thou, indeed?
70 *Tyrrel* Prove[28] me, my gracious lord.
    Richard Dar'st thou resolve to kill a friend of mine?
    Tyrrel Please you.[29] But I had rather kill two enemies.
    Richard Why then thou hast it. Two deep enemies,
      Foes to my rest and my sweet sleep's disturbers
75   Are they that I would have thee deal upon.

24 Clarence's son
25 are procrastinating, mooning about
26 about it = go do it
27 stands me much upon = matters very much / is very important to me
28 test, try
29 please you = as you like / wish

136

Tyrrel, I mean those bastards in the Tower.

Tyrrel   Let me have open means[30] to come to them,

And soon I'll rid you from the fear of them.

Richard   Thou sing'st sweet music. Hark, come hither,

Tyrrel.

Go by this token.[31] Rise, and lend thine ear.   80

(*whispers*) There is no more but so. Say it is done,

And I will love thee, and prefer thee for it.

Tyrrel   I will dispatch it straight.

EXIT TYRREL

ENTER BUCKINGHAM

Buckingham My Lord, I have considered in my mind

The late request that you did sound me in.   85

Richard   Well, let that rest. Dorset is[32] fled to Richmond.

Buckingham I hear the news, my lord.

Richard   (*to Stanley*) Stanley, he[33] is your wife's son. Well,

look unto it.

Buckingham My lord, I claim the gift, my due by promise,

For which your honor and your faith is pawned,[34]   90

Th'earldom of Hereford, and the movables

The which you promised I should possess.

Richard   Stanley, look to your wife. If she convey[35]

Letters to Richmond, you shall answer it.

Buckingham What says your Highness to my just demand?   95

30 method, way★
31 by this token = by means of this sign (e.g., a ring or some such)
32 has
33 the Earl of Richmond
34 pledged
35 transmit

Richard   I do remember me, Henry the Sixth
Did prophesy that Richmond should be king,
When Richmond was a little peevish boy.
A king, perhaps, perhaps –

100 *Buckingham* My lord –

Richard   How chance the prophet could not at that time
Have told me, I being by, that I should kill him?

Buckingham My lord, your promise for the earldom –

Richard   Richmond! When last I was at Exeter,

105 The Mayor in courtesy showed me the castle,
And called it Rouge-mont, at which name I started,
Because a bard of Ireland told me once
I should not live long after I saw Richmond.

Buckingham My lord –

110 *Richard*   Aye, what's o'clock?

Buckingham I am thus bold to put your grace in mind
Of what you promised me.

Richard   Well, but what's o'clock?

Buckingham Upon the stroke of ten.

Richard   Well, let it strike.

Buckingham Why let it strike?

115 *Richard*   Because that, like a Jack, thou keep'st[36] the stroke
Betwixt thy begging and my meditation.
I am not in the giving vein today.

Buckingham May it please you to resolve me in my suit.

Richard   Thou troublest me, I am not in the vein.

EXEUNT ALL BUT BUCKINGHAM

36 intercept, block

Buckingham Is it thus? Repays he my deep service   120
    With such contempt? Made I him king for this?
    O let me think on Hastings, and be gone
    To Brecknock,[37] while my fearful head is on!

EXIT

37 Buckingham family estate in Wales

SCENE 3

The palace

ENTER TYRREL

Tyrrel The tyrannous and bloody act is done,
  The most arch deed of piteous massacre
  That ever yet this land was guilty of.
  Dighton[1] and Forrest, whom I did suborn[2]
5 To do this ruthless piece of butchery,
  Albeit they were flesh'd villains, bloody dogs,[3]
  Melting with tenderness and mild compassion
  Wept like to children, in their deaths' sad story.
  "O thus" (quoth Dighton) "lay the gentle babes."
10 "Thus, thus" (quoth Forrest) "girdling[4] one another
  Within their alabaster[5] innocent arms.
  Their lips were four red roses on a stalk,
  And in their summer[6] beauty kissed each other.
  A book of prayers[7] on their pillow lay,
15 Which one" (quoth Forrest) "almost changed my mind.
  But O the devil" – There the villain stopped,
  Whilst Dighton thus told on: "We smothered
  The most replenishèd[8] sweet work of Nature,
  That from[9] the prime[10] creation e'er she framed."

1 DEYEtin
2 bribe, unlawfully procure / induce
3 alBEET they WERE fleshed VILlains BLOODy DOGS
4 wrapped around
5 smooth, pure white
6 young
7 bisyllabic
8 perfect
9 from the time of
10 first, original

Thence both[11] are gone with conscience and remorse,   20
They could not speak, and so I left them both,
To bring this tidings to the bloody King.
And here he comes.

ENTER RICHARD

                 All health, my sovereign lord.
Richard Kind Tyrrel, am I happy in thy news?
Tyrrel   If to have done the thing you gave in charge   25
    Beget your happiness, be happy then,
    For it is done.
Richard But didst thou see them dead?
Tyrrel   I did, my lord.
Richard   And buried, gentle Tyrrel?
Tyrrel   The chaplain of the Tower hath buried them,   30
    But where (to say the truth) I do not know.
Richard Come to me Tyrrel soon, and after supper,
    When thou shalt tell the process[12] of their death.
    Meantime, but think how I may do thee good,
    And be inheritor[13] of thy desire.   35
    Farewell till soon.
Tyrrel   I humbly take my leave.

EXIT TYRREL

The son of Clarence have I pent up close,
His daughter meanly have I matched in marriage,
The sons of Edward sleep in Abraham's bosom,[14]

---

11 i.e., Dighton and Forrest
12 course, events★
13 be inheritor = become the possessor
14 Abraham's bosom = paradise

40 And Anne my wife hath bid this world good night.
Now, for[15] I know the Breton[16] Richmond aims
At young Elizabeth, my brother's daughter,
And by that knot[17] looks proudly oe'er the crown,[18]
To her I go, a jolly thriving wooer.

ENTER RATCLIFF

45 *Ratcliff* My lord.
Richard Good or bad news, that thou comest in so bluntly?
Ratcliff Bad news, my lord. Morton[19] is fled to Richmond,
And Buckingham, backed with[19] the hardy Welshmen,
Is in the field, and still his power[20] increaseth.
50 *Richard* Ely with Richmond troubles me more near
Than Buckingham and his rash-levied[21] strength.
Come, I have learned that fearful commenting
Is leaden servitor to dull delay.
Delay leads impotent and snail-paced beggary.
55 Then fiery expedition[22] be my wing,
Jove's Mercury, and herald for a king!
Go muster men. My counsel is my shield,
We must be brief when traitors brave[23] the field.

EXEUNT

15 because
16 an insult, not a factual statement
17 marriage
18 looks proudly o'er the crown = scrutinizes the crown grandly/arrogantly
19 by
20 army★
21 rash-levied = hastily raised
22 speedy performance★
23 challenge★

SCENE 4

The palace

ENTER QUEEN MARGARET

Margaret   So now prosperity begins to mellow
  And drop into the rotten mouth of death.
  Here in these confines slily have I lurked,
  To watch the waning of mine enemies.
  A dire induction am I witness to,   5
  And will[1] to France, hoping the consequence
  Will prove as[2] bitter, black, and tragical.
  Withdraw thee, wretched Margaret. Who comes here?

ENTER QUEEN ELIZABETH AND THE DUCHESS OF YORK

Elizabeth   Ah my poor princes! Ah my tender babes!
  My unblown[3] flowers, new-appearing sweets!   10
  If yet your gentle souls fly in the air
  And be not fixed in doom[4] perpetual,
  Hover about me with your airy wings
  And hear your mother's lamentation!
Margaret   *(aside)* Hover about her, say that right for right[5]   15
  Hath dimmed your infant morn to agèd night.
Duchess of York So many miseries have crazed[6] my voice
  That my woe-wearied tongue is mute and dumb.
  Edward Plantagenet, why art thou dead?

1 will go to
2 just as, equally
3 unopened
4 decree, judgment*
5 i.e., one claim contending with another
6 shattered, crushed

20 *Margaret*   (*aside*) Plantagenet doth quit[7] Plantagenet.
               Edward for Edward[8] pays a dying debt.

    Elizabeth   Wilt thou, O God, fly from such gentle lambs,
               And throw them in the entrails of the wolf?
               When didst thou sleep when such a deed was done?

25 *Margaret*   (*aside*) When holy Harry died, and my sweet son.

    Duchess of York Dead life, blind sight, poor mortal living ghost,
               Woe's scene, world's shame, grave's due by life usurped,
               Brief abstract[9] and record of tedious days,
               Rest thy unrest on England's lawful earth
30   (*sitting*) Unlawfully made drunk with innocent blood.

    Elizabeth   Ah that thou wouldst as soon afford a grave
               As thou canst yield a melancholy seat!
               Then would I hide my bones, not rest them here.
               Ah who hath any cause to mourn but we?

SITTING DOWN BY HER

35 *Margaret*   (*coming forward*) If ancient sorrow be most
               reverend,
               Give mine the benefit of seigniory,[10]
               And let my griefs frown on the upper hand.
               (*sitting with them*) If sorrow can admit society,
               Tell o'er your woes again by viewing mine.
40   I had an Edward, till a Richard killed him.
               I had a husband, till a Richard killed him.
               Thou hadst an Edward, till a Richard killed him.

---

7 redeem, repay★
8 Edward IV's young son for Edward, Henry VI's son
9 (noun) brief abstract = short account/summary (abSTRACT)
10 primacy

Thou hadst a Richard, till a Richard killed him.
Duchess of York I had a Richard too, and thou didst kill him.

I had a Rutland too, thou holp'st to kill him.   45
Margaret   Thou hadst a Clarence too, and Richard
killed him.

From forth the kennel of thy womb hath crept
A hell-hound that doth hunt us all to death.
That dog, that had his teeth before his eyes,
To worry lambs and lap their gentle blood,   50
That foul defacer of God's handiwork,
That excellent grand tyrant of the earth,
That reigns in gallèd[11] eyes of weeping souls,
Thy womb let loose, to chase us to our graves.
O upright, just, and true-disposing God,   55
How do I thank thee, that this carnal[12] cur
Preys on the issue of his mother's body,
And makes her pew-fellow with others' moan!
Duchess of York O Harry's wife, triumph not in my woes!
God witness with me, I have wept for thine.   60
Margaret   Bear with me. I am hungry for revenge,
And now I cloy[13] me with beholding it.
Thy Edward he is dead, that stabbed my Edward,
The other Edward dead, to quit my Edward.
Young York, he is but boot,[14] because both they[15]   65
Matched not the high perfection of my loss.

11 swollen
12 carnivorous, murderous, bloody
13 overload, surfeit
14 something tossed in, an addition of no particular weight or significance
15 both they = the two sons of Edward IV

Thy Clarence he is dead, that stabbed my Edward,
And the beholders of this frantic play[16] –
Th'adulterate[17] Hastings, Rivers, Vaughan, Grey –
70   Untimely smothered[18] in their dusky graves.
Richard yet lives, hell's black intelligencer,[19]
Only reserved[20] their[21] factor to buy souls
And send them thither. But at hand,[22] at hand,
Ensues[23] his piteous and unpitied end,
75   Earth gapes, hell burns, fiends roar, saints pray,
To have him suddenly conveyed from hence.
Cancel his bond of life, dear God I pray,
That I may live and say the dog is dead!
Elizabeth   O thou didst prophesy the time would come
80   That I should wish for thee to help me curse
That bottled spider, that foul bunch-backed toad![24]
Margaret   I called thee then vain flourish of my fortune.
I called thee then poor shadow, painted queen,
The presentation[25] of but what I was –
85   The flattering index of a direful pageant,
One heaved a-high, to be hurled down below,[26]
A mother only mocked with two fair babes,

16 action, live show
17 adulterous
18 silenced, suppressed, covered
19 spy, agent
20 kept in employment / alive
21 i.e., Hell's
22 at hand = close by
23 follows, pursues
24 that BOTtled SPIder THAT foul BUNCHbacked TOAD
25 representation, picture, show
26 one HEAVED aHIGH to BE hurled DOWN beLOW

A dream of what thou wast, a garish[27] flag
To be the aim of every dangerous shot,
A figure of dignity, a breath, a bubble,   90
A queen in jest, only to fill[28] the scene.
Where is thy husband now? Where be thy brothers?
Where be thy two sons? Wherein dost thou joy[29]?
Who sues, and kneels, and says, "God save the Queen"?
Where be the bending[30] peers that flattered thee?   95
Where be the thronging[31] troops that followed thee?
Decline[32] all this, and see what now thou art.
For happy wife, a most distressèd widow,
For joyful mother, one that wails the name,
For one being sued to, one that humbly sues,   100
For queen, a very caitiff[33] crowned with care,
For she that scorned at me, now scorned of me,
For she being feared of all, now fearing one,
For she commanding all, obeyed of none.
Thus hath the course of justice whirled about,   105
And left thee but a very prey to time,
Having no more but thought of what thou wast
To torture thee the more, being what thou art.
Thou didst usurp my place, and dost thou not
Usurp the just proportion of my sorrow?   110
Now thy proud neck bears half my burthened yoke,

27 gaudy, crudely / excessively bright
28 complete, finish
29 (verb)
30 bowing
31 assembled in large numbers
32 (1) turn from, (2) recite, analyze (as in grammar)
33 wretch

From which even here I slip my weary neck
And leave the burthen of it all on thee.
Farewell, York's wife, and queen of sad mischance.

115   These English woes will make me smile in France.

Elizabeth   O thou well skilled in curses, stay awhile,
And teach me how to curse mine enemies.

Margaret   Forbear to sleep the night, and fast the day.
Compare dead happiness with living woe.

120   Think that thy babes were fairer than they were,
And he that slew them fouler than he is.
Bett'ring thy loss makes the bad causer[34] worse.
Revolving this will teach thee how to curse.

Elizabeth   My words are dull, O quicken them with thine!

125 *Margaret*   Thy woes will make them sharp, and pierce
like mine.

EXIT QUEEN MARGARET

Duchess of York   Why should[35] calamity be full of words?

Elizabeth   Windy attorneys to their client woes,
Airy succeeders of intestate joys,
Poor breathing orators of miseries,

130   Let them have scope, though what they will impart
Help nothing else, yet do they ease the heart.

Duchess of York   If so then, be not tongue-tied. Go with me,
And in the breath of bitter words let's smother
My damnèd son, that thy two sweet sons smothered.[36]

135   The trumpet sounds, be copious in exclaims.

---

34 responsible party
35 must
36 my DAMned SON that THY two SWEET sons SMOthered

ENTER RICHARD, WITH HIS ATTENDANTS

Richard	Who intercepts[37] my expedition?
Duchess of York	O she that might have intercepted thee

    (By strangling thee in her accursèd womb)

    From all the slaughters, wretch, that thou hast done!

Elizabeth   Hid'st thou that forehead with a golden crown,   140

    Where should be graven, if that right were right,

    The slaughter of the prince that owed[38] that crown,

    And the dire death of my two sons and brothers?

    Tell me, thou villain slave, where are my children?

Duchess of York Thou toad, thou toad, where is thy brother   145

    Clarence?

    And little Ned Plantagenet, his son?

Elizabeth   Where is the gentle Rivers, Vaughan,[39] Grey?

Richard   A flourish, trumpets, strike alarum, drums!

    Let not the heavens hear these tell-tale[40] women

    Rail on[41] the Lord's anointed. Strike, I say!   150

FLOURISH, ALARUMS

    Either be patient, and entreat me fair,

    Or with the clamorous report[42] of war

    Thus will I drown your exclamations.

Duchess of York Art thou my son?

Richard   Aye, I thank God, my father, and yourself.   155

Duchess of York Then patiently hear my impatience.

37 stops, interrupts
38 owned
39 bisyllabic (?)
40 tattling, malicious betraying chatterers
41 rail on = speak abusively of/to
42 musical sounds

Richard	Madam, I have a touch of your condition,
	Which cannot brook the accent[43] of reproof.
Duchess of York	O let me speak!
160	*Richard*	Do then, but I'll not hear.
Duchess of York	I will be mild and gentle in my speech.
Richard	And brief, good mother, for I am in haste.
Duchess of York	Art thou so hasty? I have stayed[44] for thee
	(God knows) in torment, and in agony.
165	*Richard*	And came I not at last to comfort you?
Duchess of York	No by the holy rood, thou know'st it well
	Thou cam'st on earth to make the earth my hell.
	A grievous burthen was thy birth to me,
	Tetchy[45] and wayward was thy infancy.
170		Thy schooldays frightful, desp'rate, wild, and furious,[46]
	Thy prime of manhood daring, bold, and venturous.
	Thy age confirmed,[47] proud, subtle, sly, and bloody,[48]
	More mild, but yet more harmful, kind in hatred.[49]
	What comfortable hour canst thou name
175		That ever graced me in thy company?
Richard	Faith, none, but Humphrey Hower,[50] that
	called your Grace
	To breakfast once, forth of my company.
	If I be so disgracious[51] in your eye,

43 sound
44 waited
45 peevish/short-tempered/irritable
46 frantic, raging
47 settled, firmly established
48 thy AGE conFIRMED proud Subtle SLY and BLOOdy
49 kind in hatred = inherently/naturally hateful
50 (?) perhaps a joke, the meaning of which has been lost
51 disgraceful

Let me march on and not offend you, madam.

Strike up the drum.

Duchess of York   I prithee, hear me speak.   180

Richard   You speak too bitterly.

Duchess of York   Hear me a word,

For I shall never speak to thee again.

Richard   So.

Duchess of York Either thou wilt die, by God's just ordinance,[52]

Ere from this war thou turn[53] a conqueror,   185

Or I with grief and extreme[54] age shall perish

And never look upon thy face again.

Therefore take with thee my most grievous curse,

Which in the day of battle tire thee more

Than all the complete[55] armor that thou wear'st.   190

My prayers on the[56] adverse party fight,

And there the little souls of Edward's children

Whisper[57] the spirits of thine enemies

And promise them success and victory.

Bloody thou art, bloody will be thy end.   195

Shame serves thy life, and doth thy death attend.

EXIT DUCHESS OF YORK

Elizabeth   Though far more cause, yet much less spirit
to curse

Abides in me. I say amen to all.

---

52 arrangement, decree, dispensation
53 return
54 advanced (Ekstream)
55 COMplete
56 on the = on the side of the
57 whisper to

Richard   Stay madam, I must talk a word with you.

200 *Elizabeth* I have no more sons of the royal blood
       For thee to slaughter. For[58] my daughters, Richard,
       They shall be praying nuns, not weeping queens,
       And therefore level[59] not to hit their lives.

Richard   You have a daughter called Elizabeth,

205   Virtuous and fair, royal and gracious.

Elizabeth And must she die for this? O let her live,
       And I'll corrupt her manners, stain her beauty,
       Slander myself as false to Edward's bed,
       Throw over her the veil of infamy

210   So she may live unscarred of bleeding slaughter.
       I will confess she was not Edward's daughter.

Richard   Wrong not her birth, she is a royal princess.

Elizabeth To save her life, I'll say she is not so.

Richard   Her life is safest only in her birth.

215 *Elizabeth* And only in that safety died her brothers.

Richard   Lo, at their birth good stars were opposite.

Elizabeth No, to their lives ill friends were contrary.[60]

Richard   All unavoided[61] is the doom of destiny.

Elizabeth True, when avoided[62] grace makes destiny.

220   My babes were destined to a fairer death,
       If grace had blessed thee with a fairer life.

Richard   You speak as if that I had slain my cousins.

Elizabeth Cousins[63] indeed, and by their uncle cozened[64]

58 as for
59 aim
60 CONtraREE
61 inevitable
62 rejected
63 cheated ones (pun on "cozened")
64 cheated

Of comfort, kingdom, kindred, freedom, life.

Whose hand soever lanced[65] their tender hearts,   225

Thy head (all indirectly) gave direction.

No doubt the murd'rous knife was dull and blunt

Till it was whetted on thy stone-hard heart,

To revel in the entrails of my lambs.

But[66] that still[67] use of grief makes wild grief tame,   230

My tongue should to thy ears not name my boys

Till that my nails were anchored in thine eyes,

And I, in such a desperate bay[68] of death,

Like a poor bark of sails and tackling reft,[69]

Rush all to pieces on thy rocky bosom.   235

Richard   Madam, so thrive I in my enterprise[70]

And dangerous success[71] of bloody wars,

As I intend more good to you and yours

Than ever you or yours were by me wronged.

Elizabeth What good is covered with the face of heaven,   240

To be discovered,[72] that can do me good?

Richard   Th'advancement of your children, gentle lady.

Elizabeth Up to some scaffold, there to lose their heads?

Richard   Unto the dignity and height of fortune,

The high imperial type[73] of this earth's glory.   245

Elizabeth Flatter my sorrows with report of it.

---

65 pierced
66 except
67 continual
68 projection of sea into land
69 of sails and tackling reft = of sails and rigging/tackle robbed
70 undertaking, work
71 result
72 revealed, uncovered
73 symbol

Tell me what state, what dignity, what honor,

Canst thou demise[74] to any child of mine?

Richard   Even all I have – aye, and myself and all,

250   Will I withal endow[75] a child of thine,

So[76] in the Lethe[77] of thy angry soul

Thou drown the sad remembrance of those wrongs

Which thou supposest I have done to thee.

Elizabeth   Be brief, lest that the process of thy kindness

255   Last longer telling than thy kindness' date.[78]

Richard   Then know that from my soul I love thy daughter.

Elizabeth   My daughter's mother thinks[79] it with her soul.

Richard   What do you think?

Elizabeth   That thou dost love my daughter from[80] thy soul.

260   So from thy soul's love didst thou love her brothers,

And from my heart's love I do thank thee for it.

Richard   Be not so hasty to confound my meaning.

I mean that with my soul I love thy daughter

And do intend to make her Queen of England.

265   *Elizabeth*   Well then, who dost thou mean shall be her king?

Richard   Even he that makes her queen. Who else should be?

Elizabeth   What, thou?

Richard   Even so. How think you of it?

Elizabeth   How canst thou woo her?

Richard   That would I learn of you,

74 give, convey
75 enrich, give as a dowry
76 so that
77 river in Hell, the water of which induces forgetting (LEEthee)
78 duration
79 ponders, considers
80 separately / at a distance from

As one being best acquainted with her humor.

Elizabeth And wilt thou learn of me?

Richard   Madam, with all   270
my heart.

Elizabeth Send to her, by the man that slew her brothers,
A pair of bleeding hearts. Thereon engrave
Edward and York, then haply she will weep.
Therefore[81] present to her – as sometime Margaret
Did to thy father, steeped in Rutland's blood –   275
A handkerchief, which say to her did drain
The purple sap from her sweet brother's body
And bid her dry her weeping eyes therewith.
If this inducement force her not to love,
Send her a letter of thy noble deeds,   280
Tell her thou mad'st away[82] her uncle Clarence,
Her uncle Rivers, aye and, for her sake,
Mad'st quick conveyance with[83] her good aunt Anne.

Richard   You mock me, madam, this is not the way
To win your daughter.

Elizabeth   There is no other way,   285
Unless thou couldst put on some other shape,
And not be Richard, that hath done all this.

Richard   Say that I did all this for love of her.

Elizabeth Nay then indeed she cannot choose but hate thee,
Having bought love with such a bloody spoil.[84]   290

Richard   Look, what is done cannot be now amended.

81 then, afterward
82 mad'st away = killed
83 conveyance with = removal of
84 plunder, booty, loot

Men shall deal unadvisedly sometimes,
Which after hours give leisure to repent.
If I did take the kingdom from your sons,
295   To make amends I'll give it to your daughter.
If I have killed the issue of your womb,
To quicken your increase[85] I will beget
Mine issue of your blood upon your daughter.
A grandam's name is little less in love
300   Than is the doting title of a mother,
They are as children but one step below,
Even of your mettle,[86] of your very blood,
Of all one pain, save for a night of groans
Endured of[87] her, for whom you bid[88] like sorrow.
305   Your children were vexation to your youth,
But mine shall be a comfort to your age.
The loss you have is but a son being king,
And by that loss your daughter is made queen.
I cannot make you what amends I would,
310   Therefore accept such kindness as I can.
Dorset your son, that with a fearful soul
Leads discontented steps in foreign soil,
This fair alliance quickly shall call home
To high promotions and great dignity:
315   The king that calls your beauteous daughter wife.
Familiarly shall call thy Dorset brother.
Again shall you be mother[89] to a king,

85 propagation, breeding, reproduction
86 spirit, nature
87 by
88 suffered
89 i.e., mother-in-law

And all the ruins of distressful times
Repaired with double riches of content.[90]
What? We have many goodly days to see.   320
The liquid drops of tears that you have shed
Shall come again, transformed to orient[91] pearl,
Advantaging[92] their love with interest
Of ten times double gain of happiness.
Go then (my mother), to thy daughter go,   325
Make bold her bashful years with your experience,
Prepare her ears to hear a wooer's tale.
Put in her tender heart th'aspiring[93] flame
Of golden sovereignty; acquaint the princess
With the sweet silent hours of marriage joys.   330
And when this arm of mine hath chastisèd[94]
The petty rebel, dull-brained Buckingham,
Bound with triumphant garlands will I come
And lead thy daughter to a conqueror's bed,
To whom I will retail my conquest won,   335
And she shall be sole victoress, Caesar's Caesar.
Elizabeth What were I best to say? Her father's brother
Would be her lord? Or shall I say her uncle?
Or he that slew her brothers and her uncles?
Under what title shall I woo for thee,   340
That God, the law, my honor, and her love,
Can make seem pleasing to her tender years?

90 kahnTENT
91 precious
92 adding
93 soaring, lofty
94 punished

Richard	Infer fair England's peace by this alliance.	
Elizabeth	Which she shall purchase with still[95] lasting war.	
345 *Richard*	Tell her the King, that may command, entreats.	
Elizabeth	That[96] at her hands which the King's King[97] forbids.	
Richard	Say she shall be a high and mighty queen.	
Elizabeth	To wail the title, as her mother doth.	
Richard	Say I will love her everlastingly.	
350 *Elizabeth*	But how long shall that title "ever" last?	
Richard	Sweetly in force unto her fair life's end.	
Elizabeth	But how long fairly shall her sweet life last?	
Richard	As long as heaven and nature lengthens it.	
Elizabeth	As long as hell and Richard likes of it.	
355 *Richard*	Say, I her sovereign, am her subject low.	
Elizabeth	But she, your subject, loathes such sovereignty.	
Richard	Be eloquent in my behalf to her.	
Elizabeth	An honest tale speeds best, being plainly told.	
Richard	Then plainly to her tell my loving tale.	
360 *Elizabeth*	Plain and not honest is too harsh a style.	
Richard	Your reasons are too shallow and too quick.	
Elizabeth	O no, my reasons are too deep and dead,	

Too deep and dead, poor infants, in their graves.

Harp on it still shall I, till heartstrings break.

365 *Richard* Harp not on that string, madam, that is past.

Now by[98] my George,[99] my Garter,[100] and my crown.

---

95 always, forever
96 that which he entreats
97 God (i.e., the laws against incest)
98 now by = (1) you must rely on, *or* (2) I swear by
99 St. George, 4th-c. martyr and patron saint of England
100 the chivalric Order of the Garter (the emblem of which bore an image of St. George)

Elizabeth Profaned, dishonored, and the third usurped.[101]

Richard I swear —

Elizabeth By nothing, for this is no oath:

Thy George, profaned, hath lost his holy honor;

The Garter, blemished, pawned his knightly virtue; 370

The crown, usurped, disgraced his kingly glory.

If something thou wilt swear to be believed,

Swear then by something that thou hast not wronged.

Richard Then by myself.

Elizabeth Thy self is self-misused.

Richard Now by the world —

Elizabeth 'Tis full of thy foul wrongs. 375

Richard My father's death —

Elizabeth Thy life hath it dishonored.

Richard Why then, by God —

Elizabeth God's wrong is most of all.

If thou didst fear to break an oath with him,

The unity the King my husband made

Thou hadst not broken, nor my brothers died. 380

If thou hadst feared to break an oath by him

Th'imperial metal, circling now thy brow,

Had graced the tender temples of my child,

And both the Princes had been breathing here,

Which now, two tender playfellows to dust, 385

Thy broken faith hath made a prey for worms.

What canst thou swear by now?

Richard The time to come.

Elizabeth That thou hast wrongèd in the time o'er past,

101 you profane St. George, dishonor the Garter, and have usurped the crown

For I myself have many tears to wash

390   Hereafter[102] time, for time past wronged by thee.

The parents live, whose children thou hast butchered,

Ungoverned[103] youth, to wail it with their age,

Old barren plants, to wail it with their age.

Swear not by time to come, for that thou hast

395   Misused ere used,[104] by time misused o'er[105] past.

Richard As I intend to prosper, and repent,

So thrive I in my dangerous affairs

Of hostile arms. Myself, myself confound!

Heaven and fortune bar me happy hours!

400   Day, yield me not thy light, nor night, thy rest!

Be opposite all planets of good luck

To my proceedings, if with pure heart's love,

Immaculate[106] devotion, holy thoughts,

I tender[107] not thy beauteous princely daughter!

405   In her consists[108] my happiness, and thine.

Without her, follows to myself, and thee,

Herself, the land, and many a Christian soul,

Death, desolation, ruin, and decay.

It cannot be avoided but by this.

410   It will not be avoided but by this.

Therefore, dear mother (I must call you so),

Be the attorney of my love to her.

102 future
103 unguided
104 ere used = before it is/can be used
105 in the
106 pure, spotless
107 care for
108 exists, lies

Plead[109] what I will be, not what I have been,

Not my deserts, but what I will deserve.

Urge the necessity and state of times,   415

And be not peevish found in great designs.

Elizabeth Shall I be tempted of the devil thus?

Richard   Aye, if the devil tempt thee to do good.

Elizabeth Shall I forget myself, to be myself?

Richard   Aye, if yourself's remembrance wrong yourself.   420

Elizabeth But thou didst kill my children.

Richard   But in your daughter's womb I bury them,

Where in that nest of spicery[110] they will breed

Selves of themselves, to your recomforture.[111]

Elizabeth Shall I go win my daughter to thy will?   425

Richard   And be a happy mother by the deed.

Elizabeth I go. Write to me very shortly,

And you shall understand from me her mind.

Richard   Bear her my true love's kiss, and so farewell.

EXIT QUEEN ELIZABETH

Relenting[112] fool, and shallow, changing woman!   430

ENTER RATCLIFF, CATESBY FOLLOWING

How now! what news?

Ratcliff   Most mighty sovereign, on the western coast

Rideth a puissant[113] navy. To our shores

---

109 (1) argue, as in a court of law, (2) beg

110 nest of spicery = the Phoenix's nest (mythical bird that reproduced by
    burning its old self in a perfumed fire)

111 consolation

112 melting, soft-minded

113 powerful★

Throng many doubtful hollow-hearted friends,
435   Unarmed, and unresolved to beat them back.
'Tis thought that Richmond is their admiral.
And there they hull,[114] expecting but the aid
Of Buckingham to welcome them ashore.
Richard   Some light-foot friend post to the Duke of Norfolk.
440   Ratcliff, thyself, or Catesby; where is he?
Catesby   Here, my good lord.
Richard   Catesby, fly to the Duke.
Catesby   I will, my lord, with all convenient[115] haste.
Richard   (*to Ratcliff*) Post thou to Salisbury
When thou comest thither – (*to Catesby*) Dull, unmindful villain,
445   Why stay'st thou here, and go'st not to the Duke?
Catesby   First, mighty liege, let me know your mind,
What from your Grace I shall deliver[116] to him.
Richard   O true, good Catesby, bid him levy[117] straight
The greatest strength and power he can make,
450   And meet me presently at Salisbury.
Catesby   I go.

EXIT CATESBY

Ratcliff   What, may it please you, shall I do at Salisbury?
Richard   Why, what wouldst thou do there, before I go?
Ratcliff   Your Highness told me I should post before.
Richard   My mind is changed.

114 float
115 suitable
116 say
117 raise, conscript

ENTER STANLEY

                    Stanley, what news with you?   455

Stanley None, good my liege, to please you with the hearing,
    Nor none so bad, but well may well be reported.

Richard Hoyday,[118] a riddle, neither good nor bad!
    What needst thou run so many miles about,
    When thou mayst tell thy tale the nearest way?   460
    Once more, what news?

Stanley   Richmond is on the seas.

Richard There let him sink, and be the seas on him!
    White-livered runagate,[119] what doth he there?

Stanley I know not, mighty sovereign, but by guess.

Richard Well, as you guess?   465

Stanley Stirred up by Dorset, Buckingham, and Morton,
    He makes for England, here to claim the crown.

Richard Is the chair[120] empty? Is the sword unswayed?[121]
    Is the King dead? The empire unpossessed?
    What heir of York is there alive but we?   470
    And who is England's king, but great York's heir?
    Then tell me, what makes he upon the seas?

Stanley Unless for that, my liege, I cannot guess.

Richard Unless for that he comes to be your liege,
    You cannot guess wherefore the Welshman comes.   475
    Thou wilt revolt, and fly to him, I fear.

Stanley No, my good lord, therefore mistrust me not.

Richard Where is thy power then, to beat him back?

118 exclamation
119 white-livered runagate = cowardly runaway / deserter
120 throne*
121 unwielded

Where be thy tenants, and thy followers?

480 Are they not now upon the western shore,

Safe-conducting the rebels from their ships?

Stanley   No, my good lord, my friends are in the north.

Richard   Cold friends to me. What do they in the north,

When they should serve their sovereign in the west?

485 *Stanley*   They have not been commanded, mighty King.

Pleaseth your Majesty to give me leave,

I'll muster up my friends, and meet your Grace

Where and what time your Majesty shall please.

Richard   Aye, thou wouldst be gone to join with Richmond.

But I'll not trust thee.

490 *Stanley*   Most mighty sovereign,

You have no cause to hold my friendship doubtful.

I never was, nor never will be false.

Richard   Go then, and muster men. But leave behind

Your son, George Stanley. Look your faith be firm,

495 Or else his head's assurance[122] is but frail.

Stanley   So deal with him, as I prove true to you.

EXIT STANLEY

ENTER A MESSENGER

Messenger My gracious sovereign, now in Devonshire,

As I by friends am well advertised,[123]

Sir Edward Courtney and the haughty prelate,

500 Bishop of Exeter, his elder brother,

With many more confederates, are in arms.

122 security, guarantee
123 notified

ENTER MESSENGER 2

Messenger 2 In Kent, my liege, the Guilfords[124] are in arms,
    And every hour[125] more competitors[126]
    Flock to the rebels, and their power grows strong.

ENTER MESSENGER 3

Messenger 3 My lord, the army of the Duke of Buckingham –   505
Richard   Out on you, owls,[127] nothing but songs of death?
    (*striking him*) There, take thou that, until thou bring better
    news.
Messenger 3 The news I have to tell your Majesty
    Is, that by sudden floods and fall of waters,[128]
    Buckingham's army is dispersed and scattered,   510
    And he himself wandered away alone,
    No man knows whither.
Richard   I cry thee mercy.
    There is my purse, to cure that blow of thine.
    Hath any well-advisèd friend proclaimed
    Reward to him that brings the traitor in?   515
Messenger 3 Such proclamation hath been made, my liege.

ENTER MESSENGER 4

Messenger 4 Sir Thomas Lovel and Lord Marquis Dorset,
    'Tis said my liege, in Yorkshire are in arms.
    But this good comfort bring I to your Highness,

124 family name
125 OWer
126 associates
127 dullards
128 i.e., rain

520 The Breton navy is dispersed by tempest.

Richmond, in Dorsetshire, sent out a boat

Unto the shore, to ask those on the banks

If they were his assistants,[129] yea or no?

Who answered him, they came from Buckingham

525 Upon his party. He, mistrusting them,

Hoised[130] sail and made his course again for Breton.

Richard March on, march on, since we are up in arms,

If not to fight with foreign enemies

Yet to beat down these rebels here at home.

ENTER CATESBY

530 Catesby My liege, the Duke of Buckingham is taken,

That is the best news. That the Earl of Richmond

Is with a mighty power landed at Milford

Is colder news, yet they must be told.

Richard Away toward Salisbury! While we reason here

535 A royal battle might be won and lost.

Some one take order Buckingham be brought

To Salisbury, the rest march on with me.

FLOURISH

EXEUNT

129 promoters, auxiliaries
130 hoisted

SCENE 5

Lord Stanley's house

ENTER STANLEY AND SIR CHRISTOPHER URSWICK

Stanley   Sir Christopher, tell Richmond this from me,
That in the sty of this most bloody boar
My son George Stanley is franked up in hold.
If I revolt, off goes young George's head,
The fear of that withholds my present aid.   5
But tell me, where is princely Richmond now?

Christopher At Pembroke, or at Harford-west, in Wales.

Stanley   What men of name[1] resort to him?

Christopher Sir Walter Herbert, a renownèd soldier,
Sir Gilbert Talbot, Sir William Stanley,   10
Oxford, redoubted[2] Pembroke, Sir James Blunt,
And Rice ap Thomas, with a valiant crew,
And many more of noble fame and worth.
And toward[3] London they do bend their power,
If by the way they be not fought withal.   15

Stanley   Well hie thee to thy lord. I kiss his hand,
My letter will resolves him of my mind.
Farewell.

EXEUNT

1 rank, dignity
2 respected, distinguished
3 TOward

Act 5

SCENE I

Salisbury, An open place

ENTER BUCKINGHAM, WITH SHERIFF AND GUARDS,
LED TO EXECUTION

Buckingham Will not King Richard let me speak with him?

Sheriff No, my good lord, therefore be patient.

Buckingham Hastings, and Edward's children, Grey and Rivers,
Holy King Henry, and thy fair son Edward,

5   Vaughan, and all that have miscarried
By underhand corrupted foul injustice,
If that your moody[1] discontented souls
Do through the clouds behold this present hour,
Even for revenge mock my destruction.

10   This is All-Souls' day[2] (fellow), is it not?

Sheriff It is.

Buckingham Why then All-Souls' day is my body's doomsday.

---

1 proud, bold
2 day of prayers for the dead

This is the day which in King Edward's time
I wished might fall on me, when[3] I was found
False to his children, and his wife's allies.   15
This is the day wherein I wished to fall
By the false faith of him whom most I trusted.
This, this All-Souls' day to my fearful soul
Is the determined respite[4] of my wrongs.
That high All-Seer which I dallied with   20
Hath turned my feignèd prayer on my head,
And given in earnest what I begged in jest.
Thus doth he force the swords of wicked men
To turn their own points on their masters' bosoms.
Now Margaret's curse falls heavy on my neck.   25
"When he," quoth she, "shall split thy heart with sorrow,
Remember Margaret was a prophetess."
Come lead me, officers, to the block of shame,
Wrong hath but wrong, and blame the due of blame.

EXEUNT

---

3 if
4 determined respite = predetermined time to end the postponement of
  punishment

SCENE 2

Camp near Tamworth

<small>ENTER RICHMOND, OXFORD, BLUNT, HERBERT,
AND OTHERS, WITH DRUM AND COLORS[1]</small>

Richmond Fellows[2] in arms, and my most loving friends,
    Bruised underneath the yoke of tyranny,
    Thus far into the bowels of the land
    Have we marched on without impediment.[3]
5   And here receive we from our father[4] Stanley
    Lines of fair comfort and encouragement.
    The wretched, bloody, and usurping boar,
    That spoiled[5] your summer fields and fruitful vines,
    Swills[6] your warm blood like wash, and makes his trough
10   In your emboweled[7] bosoms, this foul swine
    Is now even in the center of this isle,
    Near to the town of Leicester, as we learn.
    From Tamworth thither is but one day's march.
    In God's name cheerly on, courageous friends,
15   To reap the harvest of perpetual peace
    By this one bloody trial[8] of sharp war.
Oxford   Every man's conscience is a thousand men
    To fight against this guilty homicide.

1 flags, banners
2 comrades
3 obstruction, hindrance
4 stepfather
5 despoiled, stripped
6 spills out
7 disemboweled
8 test, combat

Herbert   I doubt not but his friends will turn to us.
Blunt   He hath no friends but who are friends for fear,   20
    Which in his greatest need will fly from him.
Richmond All for our vantage. Then in God's name march,
    True hope is swift, and flies with swallow's wings.
    Kings it makes gods, and meaner creatures kings.

EXEUNT

SCENE 3

Bosworth field

<small>ENTER KING RICHARD III IN ARMOR, WITH NORFOLK,
SURREY, AND OTHERS</small>

Richard Here pitch our tent, even here in Bosworth field.
　　My Lord of Surrey, why look you so sad?
Surrey　My heart is ten times lighter than my looks.
Richard My Lord of Norfolk.
5　*Norfolk* Here, most gracious liege.
　　Richard Norfolk, we must have knocks.[1] Ha, must we not?
　　Norfolk We must both give and take, my loving lord.
　　Richard Up with my tent there, here will I lie tonight,
　　But where tomorrow? Well, all's one for that.[2]
10　Who hath descried[3] the number of the traitors?
　　Norfolk Six or seven thousand is their utmost power.
　　Richard Why, our battalia[4] trebles that account.
　　Besides, the King's name is a tower of strength,
　　Which they upon the adverse party want.[5]
15　Up with the tent there. Come, noble gentlemen,
　　Let us survey the vantage of the ground.[6]
　　Call for some men of sound direction.[7]
　　Let's lack no discipline, make no delay,
　　For lords, tomorrow is a busy day.

---

1 rebuffs, misfortunes, setbacks ("hard thumps")
2 all's one for that = it makes no difference
3 discovered
4 armed force
5 lack
6 i.e., where the best/most advantageous position lies
7 ability to take command

ACT 5 • SCENE 3

EXEUNT (THE TENT REMAINS)

ENTER ON THE OTHER SIDE OF THE STAGE RICHMOND,
SIR WILLIAM BRANDON, OXFORD, AND OTHERS,
WHO PITCH RICHMOND'S TENT

Richmond The weary sun hath made a golden set,[8]   20
  And by the bright tract[9] of his fiery car
  Gives signal of a goodly day tomorrow.
  Sir William Brandon, you shall bear my standard.[10]
  Give me some ink and paper in my tent.
  I'll draw the form and model of our battle,   25
  Limit each leader to his several charge,
  And part in just proportion our small power.
  My Lord of Oxford, you Sir William Brandon,
  And you Sir Walter Herbert stay with me.
  The Earl of Pembroke keeps[11] his regiment.[12]   30
  Good Captain Blunt, bear my good night to him,
  And by the second hour in the morning
  Desire the Earl to see me in my tent.
  Yet one thing more (good captain) do for me.
  Where is Lord Stanley quartered, do you know?   35
Blunt   Unless I have mista'en his colors[13] much
  (Which well I am assured I have not done),
  His regiment lies half a mile at least
  South from the mighty power of the King.

8 setting
9 process, course
10 flag, banner
11 will keep charge of
12 fairly large body of troops
13 flags, banners

40 *Richmond* If without peril it be possible,

   Sweet Blunt, make some good means to speak with him

   And give him from me this most needful note.

 Blunt Upon my life, my lord, I'll undertake it,

   And so God give you quiet rest tonight.

45 *Richmond* Good night, good Captain Blunt. Come gentlemen,

   Let us consult upon tomorrow's business.

   Into my tent, the dew is raw and cold.

THEY WITHDRAW INTO THE TENT[14]

ENTER RICHARD, NORFOLK, RATCLIFF,
CATESBY, AND OTHERS

 Richard What is't o'clock?

 Catesby   It's supper-time my lord,

   It's nine o'clock.

 Richard   I will not sup tonight.

50 Give me some ink and paper.

   What, is my beaver easier[15] than it was?

   And all my armor laid into my tent?

 Catesby If is my liege, and all things are in readiness.

 Richard Good Norfolk, hie thee to thy charge,

55 Use careful watch, choose trusty sentinels.

 Norfolk I go my lord.

 Richard Stir with the lark tomorrow, gentle Norfolk.

 Norfolk I warrant you my lord.

EXIT NORFOLK

14 but remain on their side of the stage
15 beaver easier = lower part of my faceguard moving less stiffly

Richard Catesby.

Catesby My lord?

Richard   Send out a pursuivant-at-arms   60
   To Stanley's regiment. Bid him bring his power
   Before sunrising, lest his son George fall
   Into the blind cave of eternal night.

                    EXIT CATESBY

(*to attendants*) Fill me a bowl of wine. Give me a watch.[16]
   Saddle white Surrey[17] for the field tomorrow.   65
   Look that my staves[18] be sound, and not too heavy.
   Ratcliff.

Ratcliff My lord?

Richard Saw'st thou the melancholy Lord Northumberland?

Ratcliff Thomas the Earl of Surrey, and himself,   70
   Much about cock-shut[19] time, from troop to troop
   Went through the army, cheering up the soldiers.

Richard So, I am satisfied. Give me a bowl of wine,
   I have not that alacrity[20] of spirit,
   Nor cheer of mind, that I was wont to have.   75
   Set it down. Is ink and paper ready?

Ratcliff It is my lord.

Richard Bid my guard watch. Leave me.
   Ratcliff, about the mid of night come to my tent
   And help to arm me. Leave me, I say.[21]   80

16 sentinels, watchmen
17 horse's name
18 lance shafts
19 twilight
20 liveliness, readiness
21 Richard remains in his tent, on his side of the stage, and falls asleep

EXEUNT RATCLIFF AND OTHER ATTENDANTS

ENTER STANLEY TO RICHMOND'S TENT,
LORDS AND OTHERS ATTENDING

Stanley   Fortune and victory sit on thy helm!
Richmond All comfort that the dark night can afford
    Be to thy person, noble father-in-law.
    Tell me, how fares our loving mother?
85 *Stanley*   I by attorney[22] bless thee from thy mother,
    Who prays continually for Richmond's good.
    So much for that. The silent hours steal on,
    And flaky[23] darkness breaks within the east.
    In brief, for so the season bids us be,
90   Prepare thy battle early in the morning,
    And put thy fortune to the arbitrament[24]
    Of bloody strokes and mortal-staring[25] war.
    I, as I may (that which I would I cannot),
    With best advantage will deceive the time,[26]
95   And aid thee in this doubtful shock[27] of arms.
    But on thy side I may not be too forward
    Lest being seen, thy brother, tender George,
    Be executed in his father's sight.
    Farewell. The leisure[28] and the fearful time
100   Cuts off the ceremonious vows of love

22 by his wife's deputation
23 cracking, flaking, streaked with light
24 decision ("arbitration")
25 mortal-staring = fatally staring
26 moment
27 encounter
28 allowed time

And ample interchange of sweet discourse,
Which so long sundered[29] friends should dwell upon.
God give us leisure for these rites of love.
Once more adieu, be valiant, and speed well!
Richmond Good lords, conduct him to his regiment.   105
  I'll strive with[30] troubled thoughts to take a nap,
  Lest leaden slumber peise[31] me down tomorrow,
  When I should mount with wings of victory.
  Once more, good night, kind lords and gentlemen.

EXEUNT ALL BUT RICHMOND

O Thou, whose captain[32] I account[33] myself,   110
Look on my forces with a gracious eye.
Put in their hands thy bruising irons[34] of wrath,
That they may crush down with a heavy fall
Th'usurping helmets of our adversaries!
Make us thy ministers of chastisement,   115
That we may praise thee in the victory.
To thee I do commend my watchful soul,
Ere I let fall the windows of mine eyes.
Sleeping, and waking, O defend me still.

HE SLEEPS

ENTER GHOST OF PRINCE EDWARD, HENRY VI'S SON

29 separated
30 against
31 weigh
32 prince, general
33 count, enumerate
34 instruments, tools

120 *Edward's Ghost* (*to Richard*) Let me sit heavy on thy soul
tomorrow.
Think how thou stab'dst me in my prime of youth
At Tewkesbury. Despair therefore, and die!
(*to Richmond*) Be cheerful Richmond, for the wrongèd souls
Of butchered princes fight in thy behalf.
125 King Henry's issue, Richmond, comforts thee.

ENTER GHOST OF HENRY VI

Henry's Ghost (*to Richard*) When I was mortal, my anointed
body
By thee was punchèd[35] full of deadly holes.
Think on the Tower, and me. Despair, and die!
Harry the Sixth bids thee despair, and die!
130 (*to Richmond*) Virtuous and holy, be thou conqueror.
Harry, that prophesied thou shouldst be king,
Doth comfort thee in sleep. Live, and flourish!

ENTER GHOST OF CLARENCE

Clarence's Ghost (*to Richard*) Let me sit heavy on thy soul
tomorrow.
I that was washed to death with fulsome[36] wine,
135 Poor Clarence, by thy guile betrayed to death.
Tomorrow in the battle think on me,
And fall thy edgeless sword. Despair, and die!
(*to Richmond*) Thou offspring of the house of Lancaster,
The wrongèd heirs of York do pray for thee.
140 Good angels guard thy battle. Live, and flourish!

ENTER THE GHOSTS OF RIVERS, GREY, AND VAUGHAN

35 stabbed
36 a copious supply of

Rivers' Ghost   (*to Richard*) Let me sit heavy on thy soul
    tomorrow,
  Rivers, that died at Pomfret. Despair, and die!
Gray's Ghost   (*to Richard*) Think upon Grey, and let thy soul
    despair!
Vaughan's Ghost (*to Richard*) Think upon Vaughan, and with
    guilty fear
  Let fall thy lance. Despair, and die!   145
All the Ghosts   (*to Richmond*) Awake, and think our wrongs in
    Richard's bosom
  Will conquer him. Awake, and win the day!

ENTER HASTINGS' GHOST

Hastings' Ghost   (*to Richard*) Bloody and guilty, guiltily awake,
  And in a bloody battle end thy days!
  Think on Lord Hastings. Despair, and die!   150
  (*to Richmond*) Quiet untroubled soul, awake, awake!
  Arm, fight, and conquer, for fair England's sake!

ENTER THE TWO YOUNG PRINCES' GHOSTS

Princes' Ghosts   (*to Richard*) Dream on thy cousins smothered in
    the Tower.
  Let us be laid within thy bosom, Richard,
  And weigh thee down to ruin, shame, and death,   155
  Thy nephews' souls bid thee despair and die!
  (*to Richmond*) Sleep, Richmond, sleep in peace, and wake
    in joy,
  Good angels guard thee from the boar's annoy!³⁷
  Live, and beget a happy race of kings!

37 vexation

160   Edward's unhappy[38] sons do bid thee flourish.

ENTER LADY ANNE'S GHOST

Anne's Ghost   (*to Richard*) Richard, thy wife, that wretched
        Anne thy wife,
        That never slept a quiet hour with thee,
        Now fills thy sleep with perturbations.
        Tomorrow in the battle think on me,
165   And fall thy edgeless sword. Despair, and die!
        (*to Richmond*) Thou quiet soul, sleep thou a quiet sleep.
        Dream of success and happy victory,
        Thy adversary's wife doth pray for thee.

ENTER BUCKINGHAM'S GHOST

Buckingham's Ghost (*to Richard*) The first was I that helped thee
        to the crown.
170   The last was I that felt thy tyranny.
        O in the battle think on Buckingham,
        And die in terror of thy guiltiness!
        Dream on, dream on, of bloody deeds and death,
        Fainting, despair. Despairing, yield thy breath!
175   (*to Richmond*) I died for hope ere I could lend thee aid,
        But cheer thy heart, and be thou not dismayed.
        God, and good angels, fight on Richmond's side,
        And Richard falls in height of all his pride.

GHOSTS VANISH

RICHARD STARTS OUT OF HIS DREAM

38 miserable, unfortunate

Richard Give me another horse, bind up my wounds.

    Have mercy, Jesu! Soft, I did but dream.   180

    O coward conscience, how dost thou afflict me!

    The lights burn blue.[39] It is now dead midnight.

    Cold fateful drops stand on my trembling flesh.

    What, do I fear myself? There's none else by,

    Richard loves Richard – that is, I am I.   185

    Is there a murderer here? No. Yes, I am.

    Then fly. What, from myself? Great reason, why?

    Lest I revenge. What, myself upon myself?

    Alack, I love myself. Wherefore? For any good

    That I myself have done unto myself?   190

    O no. Alas, I rather hate myself

    For hateful deeds committed by myself.

    I am a villain. Yet I lie, I am not.

    Fool, of thyself speak well. Fool, do not flatter.

    My conscience hath a thousand several tongues,   195

    And every tongue brings in a several tale,

    And every tale condemns me for a villain.

    Perjury, perjury, in the high'st degree,

    Murder, stern murder, in the dir'st degree,

    All several sins, all used in each degree,   200

    Throng to th'bar,[40] crying all, Guilty! Guilty!

    I shall despair, there is no creature loves me,

    And if I die, no soul shall pity me.

    Nay, wherefore should they, since that I myself

    Find in myself no pity to myself?   205

39 indicative of the presence of ghosts or the devil, or as an omen of death
40 railing separating a judge from the rest of the courtroom

Methought the souls of all that I had murdered
Came to my tent, and every one did threat
Tomorrow's vengeance on the head of Richard.

ENTER RATCLIFF

Ratcliff	My lord.
210 *Richard*	Who's there?
Ratcliff	Ratcliff, my lord, 'tis I. The early village cock

Hath twice done salutation to the morn,
Your friends are up, and buckle on their armor.

Richard	O Ratcliff, I have dreamed a fearful dream.

215 What thinkest thou, will our friends prove all true?

Ratcliff	No doubt, my lord.
Richard	O Ratcliff, I fear, I fear –
Ratcliff	Nay, good my lord, be not afraid of shadows.
Richard	By the apostle Paul, shadows tonight

Have struck more terror to the soul of Richard
220 Than can the substance of ten thousand soldiers
Armed in proof,[41] and led by shallow Richmond.
'Tis not yet near day. Come go with me,
Under our tents I'll play the eavesdropper,
To hear if any mean to shrink[42] from me.

EXEUNT

ENTER LORDS TO RICHMOND, SITTING IN HIS TENT

225 *Lords*	Good morrow, Richmond.
Richmond	Cry mercy, lords and watchful gentlemen,

41 proven strength ("impenetrable")
42 withdraw, retreat

That you have ta'en a tardy sluggard here.

Lords　　How have you slept, my lord?

Richmond　The sweetest sleep, and fairest-boding[43] dreams

　　That ever entered in a drowsy head,　　　　　　　　　　230

　　Have I since your departure had, my lords.

　　Methought their souls, whose[44] bodies Richard murdered,

　　Came to my tent, and cried on[45] victory.

　　I promise you, my soul is very jocund,

　　In the remembrance of so fair a dream.　　　　　　　　　235

　　How far into the morning is it, lords?

Lords　　Upon the stroke of four.

Richmond　Why then 'tis time to arm, and give direction.

HE MAKES HIS ORATION TO HIS ARMY

　　More than I have said, loving countrymen,

　　The leisure and enforcement of the time　　　　　　　　240

　　Forbids to dwell upon. Yet remember this,

　　God, and our good cause, fight upon our side.

　　The prayers of holy saints and wrongèd souls

　　Like high-reared bulwarks[46] stand before our faces.

　　Richard except, those whom we fight against　　　　　　245

　　Had rather have us win than him they follow,

　　For what is he they follow? Truly, gentlemen,

　　A bloody tyrant and a homicide,

　　One raised in blood and one in blood established[47] –

---

43 fairest-boding = best/finest predicting
44 those whose
45 cried on = called out loud
46 high-reared bulwarks = ramparts/fortifications made tall
47 settled, fixed, confirmed

250 One that made means to come by what he hath,
And slaughtered those that were the means to help him –
A base foul stone, made precious by the foil[48]
Of England's chair,[49] where he is falsely set –
One that hath ever been God's enemy.

255 Then if you fight against God's enemy,
God will in justice ward[50] you as his soldiers.
If you do sweat[51] to put a tyrant down,
You sleep in peace, the tyrant being slain.
If you do fight against your country's foes,

260 Your country's fat[52] shall pay your pains the hire.[53]
If you do fight in safeguard of your wives,
Your wives shall welcome home the conquerors.
If you do free your children from the sword,
Your children's children quit it in your age.

265 Then in the name of God and all these rights,
Advance your standards,[54] draw your willing swords.
For me, the ransom[55] of my bold attempt
Shall be this cold corpse on the earth's cold face.
But if I thrive, the gain of my attempt

270 The least of you shall share his part thereof.
Sound drums and trumpets boldly, and cheerfully.
God and Saint George! Richmond and victory!

EXEUNT

48 backing, wrapping, setting
49 throne
50 defend, guard, protect
51 exert yourselves, toil, labor
52 abundance, riches
53 wages
54 flags, banners
55 cost, price

ENTER RICHARD, RATCLIFF, ATTENDANTS, AND SOLDIERS

Richard	What said Northumberland as touching Richmond?	
Ratcliff	That he was never trained up in arms.[56]	
Richard	He said the truth. And what said Surrey then?	275
Ratcliff	He smiled and said, "The better for our purpose."	
Richard	He was in the right, and so indeed it is.	

CLOCK STRIKES

Tell[57] the clock there. Give me a calendar.[58]
Who saw the sun today?

Ratcliff   Not I, my lord.

Richard Then he disdains to shine, for by the book[59]   280
He should have braved the east an hour ago.
A black day will it be to somebody. Ratcliff.

Ratcliff My lord?

Richard   The sun will not be seen today,
The sky doth frown and lour upon our army.
I would these dewy tears were from[60] the ground.   285
Not shine today? Why, what is that to me
More than to Richmond? For the selfsame heaven
That frowns on me looks sadly upon him.

ENTER NORFOLK

Norfolk Arm, arm, my lord. The foe vaunts[61] in the field.

Richard Come, bustle, bustle. Caparison[62] my horse.   290

56 warfare
57 count
58 almanac
59 the calendar
60 away from, off of
61 displays, acts proudly
62 harness and ornament with cloth coverings

Call up Lord Stanley, bid him bring his power,
I will lead forth my soldiers to the plain,
And thus my battle shall be ordered:
My forward shall be drawn in length,
295 Consisting equally of horse and foot,
Our archers shall be placed in the midst.
John Duke of Norfolk, Thomas Earl of Surrey,
Shall have the leading of this foot and horse.
They thus directed, we will follow
300 In the main battle, whose puissance on either side
Shall be well wingèd[63] with our chiefest horse.
This, and Saint George to boot![64] What think'st thou,
Norfolk?
 Norfolk A good direction, warlike sovereign.
 (*shows a paper*) This found I on my tent this morning.
305 *Richard* (*reading*) "Jockey[65] of Norfolk, be not so bold,
For Dickon thy master is bought and sold."[66]
A thing devisèd by the enemy.
Go gentlemen, every man unto his charge,
Let not our babbling[67] dreams affright our souls.
310 Conscience is but a word that cowards use,
Devised at first to keep the strong in awe.
Our strong arms be our conscience, swords our law.
March on, join[68] bravely, let us to't pell-mell,[69]

63 furnished with troops on either side of them
64 to boot = in addition
65 John (nickname)
66 deceived, tricked, betrayed
67 chattering, prating
68 go into combat
69 (1) in a rush, headlong, (2) at close quarters

If not to heaven, then hand in hand to hell.

HE MAKES HIS ORATION TO HIS ARMY

What shall I say more than I have inferred?   315
Remember whom you are to cope[70] withal,
A sort of vagabonds, rascals, and runaways,
A scum of Bretons, and base lackey peasants,
Whom their o'er-cloyed[71] country vomits forth
To desperate ventures and assured destruction.   320
You sleeping safe, they bring to you unrest.
You having lands, and blest with beauteous wives,
They would restrain[72] the one, distain[73] the other,
And who doth lead them, but a paltry[74] fellow,
Long kept in Bretagne[75] at our mother's cost?   325
A milksop, one that never in his life
Felt so much cold as over shoes in snow.[76]
Let's whip these stragglers o'er[77] the seas again,
Lash hence these overweening[78] rags of France,
These famished beggars, weary of their lives,   330
Who but for dreaming on this fond exploit,
For want of means – poor rats – had hanged themselves.
If we be conquered, let men conquer us,
And not these bastard Bretons, whom our fathers

70 encounter, come to blows
71 filled, populated
72 steal
73 dishonor
74 petty, contemptible, despicable
75 Brittany
76 over shoes in snow = as snow that is barely as deep as shoes
77 back over
78 arrogant

335 Have in their own land beaten, bobbed,[79] and thumped,

And on record left them the heirs of shame.

Shall these enjoy our lands? Lie with our wives?

Ravish our daughters?

DRUM AFAR OFF

Hark, I hear their drum.

Right gentlemen of England, fight boldly, yeomen![80]

340 Draw archers, draw your arrows to the head!

Spur your proud horses hard, and ride in blood!

Amaze the welkin[81] with your broken staves![82]

ENTER A MESSENGER

What says Lord Stanley? Will he bring his power?

Messenger My lord, he doth deny to come.

345 *Richard*   Off with his son George's head!

Norfolk   My lord, the enemy is past the marsh.

After the battle let George Stanley die.

Richard   A thousand hearts are great within my bosom,

Advance our standards, set upon our foes.

350 Our ancient word of courage, fair Saint George,

Inspire us with the spleen of fiery dragons!

Upon them! Victory sits on our helms.

EXEUNT

79 left swollen with blows
80 freeholder, ranked just below gentlemen (YOmin)
81 amaze the welkin = stun/terrify the clouds/heavens
82 lance shafts

SCENE 4

Another part of the field

ALARUM, EXCURSIONS[1]

ENTER NORFOLK AND SOLDIERS, THEN CATESBY
AT THE OTHER SIDE OF THE STAGE

Catesby Rescue, my Lord of Norfolk, rescue, rescue!
    The King enacts more wonders than a man,
    Daring an opposite to every danger.
    His horse is slain, and all on foot he fights,
    Seeking for Richmond in the throat of death.   5
    Rescue, fair lord, or else the day is lost!

EXEUNT NORFOLK AND SOLDIERS.
ALARUMS. ENTER RICHARD

Richard A horse, a horse, my kingdom for a horse!
Catesby Withdraw my lord, I'll help you to a horse.
Richard Slave, I have set my life upon a cast,[2]
    And I will stand the hazard of the die.[3]   10
    I think there be six Richmonds in the field,
    Five have I slain today instead of him.
    A horse, a horse, my kingdom for a horse!

EXEUNT

1 soldiers running this way and that
2 throw
3 singular form of "dice"

SCENE 5

Another part of the field

ALARUM. ENTER RICHARD AND RICHMOND.
THEY FIGHT, RICHARD IS SLAIN

RETREAT AND FLOURISH. ENTER RICHMOND,
STANLEY BEARING THE CROWN, AND OTHER LORDS

Richmond God and your arms be praised, victorious friends,
 The day is ours, the bloody dog is dead.
Stanley Courageous Richmond, well hast thou acquit thee.
 Lo, here this long-usurpèd royalty[1]
5 From the dead temples of this bloody wretch
 Have I plucked off, to grace thy brows withal.
 Wear it, enjoy it, and make much of it.
Richmond Great God of heaven, say amen to all!
 But tell me, is young George Stanley living?
10 *Stanley* He is my lord, and safe in Leicester town,
 Whither (if you please) we may now withdraw us.
Richmond What men of name are slain on either side?
Stanley John Duke of Norfolk, Walter Lord Ferris,
 Sir Robert Brakenbury, and Sir William Brandon.
15 *Richmond* Inter their bodies as becomes their births,
 Proclaim a pardon to the soldiers fled,
 That in submission will return to us,
 And then as[2] we have ta'en the sacrament[3]

1 the crown as emblem/sign of royalty (Henry, Earl of Richmond = grandson
 of Catherine, widow of Henry V; she then married Owen Tudor; their son,
 and Richmond's father, Edmund Tudor, married Margaret Beaufort, lineal
 descendant of John of Gaunt)

2 just as
3 i.e., his vow to marry Elizabeth, Edward IV's youngest daughter, when he
 became king, was sanctified/verified by the religious rite

We will unite[4] the white rose and the red.[5]
Smile heaven upon this fair conjunction,   20
That[6] long have frowned upon their enmity.
What traitor hears me, and says not amen?
England hath long been mad, and scarred[7] herself.
The brother blindly shed the brother's blood,
The father rashly slaughtered his own son,   25
The son, compelled, been butcher to the sire.
All this divided York and Lancaster,
Divided in their dire division.[8]
O now, let Richmond and Elizabeth,
The true succeeders of each royal house,   30
By God's fair ordinance conjoin together.
And let their heirs, God (if thy will be so),
Enrich the time to come with smooth-faced peace,
With smiling plenty and fair prosperous days.
Abate[9] the edge[10] of traitors, gracious Lord,   35
That would reduce[11] these bloody days again,
And make poor England weep in streams of blood!
Let them not live to taste this land's increase
That would with treason wound this fair land's peace.
Now civil wounds are stopped, peace lives again.   40
That she may long live here, God say amen!

EXEUNT

4 i.e., by marriage with the Lancastrian princess Elizabeth
5 white rose = Yorkist emblem; red rose = Lancastrian emblem
6 you who
7 disfigured
8 diVIzeeOWN
9 destroy, demolish
10 sword
11 bring back

Why I, in this weak piping time of peace,
Have no delight to pass away the time,
Unless to see my shadow in the sun
And descant on mine own deformity.
And therefore, since I cannot prove a lover,
To entertain these fair well-spoken days
I am determined to prove a villain
And hate the idle pleasures of these days.

[1.1.24–31]

The opening ferocity of Richard, still duke of Gloucester, in *The Tragedy of Richard the Third* is hardly more than a fresh starting point for the development of the Elizabethan and Jacobean hero-villain after Marlowe, and yet it seems to transform Tamburlaine and Barabbas utterly. Richard's peculiarly self-conscious pleasure in his own audacity is crossed by the sense of what it means to see one's own deformed shadow in the sun. We are closer already not only to Edmund and Iago than to Barabbas, but especially closer to Webster's Lodovico who so sublimely says: "I limn'd this nightpiece and it was my best." Except for Iago, nothing seems farther advanced in this desperate mode than Webster's Bosola:

> O direful misprision!
> I will not imitate things glorious
> No more than base: I'll be mine own example. –
> On, on, and look thou represent, for silence,
> The thing thou bear'st.

> [5.4.87–91]

Iago is beyond even this denial of representation, because he does will silence: "Demand me nothing; what you know, you know: / From this time forth I never will speak word" (5.2.303–304).

Iago is no hero-villain, and no shift of perspective will make him into one. Pragmatically, the authentic hero-villain in Shakespeare might be judged to be Hamlet, but no audience would agree. Macbeth could justify the description, except that the cosmos of his drama is too estranged from any normative representation for the term *hero-villain* to have its oxymoronic coherence. Richard and Edmund would appear to be the models, beyond Marlowe, that could have inspired Webster and his fellows, but Edmund is too uncanny and superb a representation to provoke emulation. That returns us to Richard:

> Was ever woman in this humor wooed?
> Was ever woman in this humor won?
> I'll have her, but I will not keep her long.
> What? I that killed her husband, and his father,
> To take her in her heart's extremest hate,
> With curses in her mouth, tears in her eyes,

The bleeding witness of her hatred by,
Having God, her conscience, and these bars against me,
And I, no friends to back my suit withal,
But the plain devil, and dissembling looks?
And yet to win her? All the world to nothing!
Ha!
Hath she forgot already that brave prince,
Edward, her lord, whom I, some three months since,
Stabbed in my angry mood at Tewkesbury?
A sweeter and a lovelier gentleman,
Framed in the prodigality of nature,
Young, valiant, wise, and (no doubt) right royal,
The spacious world cannot again afford.
And will she yet abase her eyes on me,
That cropped the golden prime of this sweet prince,
And made her widow to a woeful bed?
On me, whose all not equals Edward's moiety?
On me, that halts, and am unshapen thus?
My dukedom to a beggarly denier,
I do mistake my person all this while.
Upon my life, she finds (although I cannot)
Myself to be a marv'lous proper man.
I'll be at charges for a looking-glass,
And entertain a score or two of tailors,
To study fashions to adorn my body.
Since I am crept in favor with myself,
I will maintain it with some little cost.
But first I'll turn yon fellow in his grave,
And then return lamenting to my love.

Shine out, fair sun, till I have bought a glass,
That I may see my shadow as I pass.

[1.2.227–263]

Richard's only earlier delight was "to see my shadow in the sun / And descant on mine own deformity." His savage delight in the success of his own manipulative rhetoric now transforms his earlier trope into the exultant command: "Shine out, fair sun, till I have bought a glass, / That I may see my shadow as I pass." That transformation is the formula for interpreting the Jacobean hero-villain and his varied progeny: Milton's Satan, the Poet in Shelley's *Alastor,* Wordsworth's Oswald in *The Borderers,* Byron's Manfred and Cain, Browning's Childe Roland, Tennyson's Ulysses, Melville's Captain Ahab, Hawthorne's Chillingworth, down to Nathanael West's Shrike in *Miss Lonelyhearts,* who perhaps ends the tradition. The manipulative, highly self-conscious, obsessed hero-villain, whether Machiavellian plotter or later, idealistic quester, ruined or not, moves himself from being the passive sufferer of his own moral and/or physical deformity to becoming a highly active melodramatist. Instead of standing in the light of nature to observe his own shadow, and then have to take his own deformity as subject, he rather commands nature to throw its light upon his own glass of representation, so that his own shadow will be visible only for an instant as he passes on to the triumph of his will over others.

Why is *Richard III* so permanently popular? If it *were* by Marlowe it would be neglected, since it is not of the eminence of the *Tamburlaine* plays, *The Jew of Malta, Edward II,* and *Faustus.* Shakespeare's energetic universalism makes it work, despite the palpable flaws. Marvelous melodrama, this play still seems to me something of another Shakespearean send-up of Marlowe, though toned down from the bloody farce of *Titus Andronicus*. I never have gotten through a performance of *Titus,* including Julie Taymor's charming film version. I *can* sit through *Richard III,* on stage or screen, but only because I have never had to endure an uncut presentation.

Setting aside Shakespeare's more-than-merited eminence, why does the public always rejoice in *Richard III?* All audiences, I suspect, are sadomasochistic *as audiences.* Inscrutably, Shakespeare appeals to that element (in which he was Marlowe's apprentice) in a range of modes from the coarse exuberance of *Titus Andronicus* to the refined Gnostic shocks of *Measure for Measure. Titus* is so outrageous that, more often than not, audiences resort to an uneasy defensive laughter. *Measure for Measure* is a subtle riddle, to be seen through a glass darkly. *Richard III,* midway in sensibility between the two, goes on satisfying the common playgoer.

My late, much-lamented friend A. D. Nuttall defended *Richard III* from my strictures, in his remarkable recent study, *Shakespeare the Thinker* (2007). For him the play is not apprentice-work, but I continue to dissent. Another astute scholar-critic, T. J. Cribb, in a recent article, finds the Shakespearean agon with Marlowe continuing in *Henry V,* as I indeed failed to realize. Cribb remarks that Shakespeare's relation to Marlowe was apprenticeship and never struggle. Shakespeare, I now believe, playfully continued in what gradually became a mock-apprentice relation to Marlowe, almost down to the end. Prospero inverts Faustus, and I cannot abandon my old conviction that something of the Marlowe-Shakespeare enemy brother relationship is slyly reworked in *King Lear,* where Edgar, Shakespeare's surrogate, at last destroys his Marlovian half-brother, Edmund the Bastard.

The English Bible, Chaucer, and Ovid doubtless were the principal long-term influences upon Shakespeare, but the ghost of Kit Marlowe never did stop haunting the greatest of all writers, ever. Without Marlowe, Shakespeare could not have gained such stunning power over all of us. *Richard III* seems to me an uneasy emulsion of tribute to Marlowe and a cheerful resentment against him. The tone of melodrama, which few playwrights consistently resolve, is cunningly handled in *Richard III.* Parody hovers nearby, but Richard's menacing charm is not primarily parodistic. You don't like Richard, but he is too scary for any audience to evade. There was still an ambiguous strain in Shakespeare's reception of the dramatist without whom the eventual creator of Iago and Macbeth could not have emerged.

Marlowe barely developed as a poet. He was murdered while still a young man, and had Shakespeare vanished at that same moment, the two playwrights might now seem equal to us. Perhaps something in Shakespeare told him, with Marlowe's death: "Now I am king of the cats," though sorrow and fear would have been mixed into his reaction as well. Nuttall is admirable but disputable in his comparison of *Richard III* to Marlowe's *The Jew of Malta:* "Shakespeare's Richard III is readily comparable with Marlowe's Jew of Malta, and Richard is the finer creation because the humor is sharper and the complex involvement of deformity with sexual prowess a sheer bonus." Marlowe's Jew, Barabbas, seems to me far wittier than Richard III. Richard's humor may be sharper, but is not particularly memorable, whereas I never forget Barabbas at his most outrageous: "Sometimes I go about a–nights and poison wells" and also Hemingway's favorite: "But that was in another country / And besides the wench is dead."

Richard III will never lack productions, and *The Jew of Malta* gets very few, but in this pairing, Marlowe wins. It was a long struggle that Shakespeare waged with Marlowe, and the high tragedies, from *Hamlet* on to *Antony and Cleopatra,* are beyond anything of which Marlowe ever could have become capable. For anyone else, *Richard III* would have been a triumph, but for Shakespeare it seems to me secondary stuff.

FURTHER READING

This is not a bibliography but a selective set of starting places.

Texts

Shakespeare, William. *The First Folio of Shakespeare,* 2d ed. Edited by
Charlton Hinman. Introduction by Peter W. M. Blayney. New York:
W. W. Norton, 1996.

——. *The First Quarto of King Richard III.* Edited by Peter Davison.
Cambridge: Cambridge University Press, 1996.

Language

Houston, John Porter. *The Rhetoric of Poetry in the Renaissance and
Seventeenth Century.* Baton Rouge: Louisiana State University Press,
1983.

——. *Shakespearean Sentences: A Study in Style and Syntax.* Baton
Rouge: Louisiana State University Press, 1988.

Kermode, Frank. *Shakespeare's Language.* New York: Farrar, Straus and
Giroux, 2000.

Kökeritz, Helge. *Shakespeare's Pronunciation.* New Haven: Yale
University Press, 1953.

Lanham, Richard A. *The Motives of Eloquence: Literary Rhetoric in the
Renaissance.* New Haven and London: Yale University Press, 1976.

Marcus, Leah S. *Unediting the Renaissance: Shakespeare, Marlowe, Milton*. London: Routledge, 1996.

The Oxford English Dictionary: Second Edition on CD-ROM, version 3.0. New York: Oxford University Press, 2002.

Raffel, Burton. *From Stress to Stress: An Autobiography of English Prosody*. Hamden, Conn.: Archon Books, 1992.

Ronberg, Gert. *A Way with Words: The Language of English Renaissance Literature*. London: Arnold, 1992.

Trousdale, Marion. *Shakespeare and the Rhetoricians*. Chapel Hill: University of North Carolina Press, 1982.

Culture

Bindoff, S. T. *Tudor England*. Baltimore: Penguin, 1950.

Bradbrook, M. C. *Shakespeare: The Poet in His World*. New York: Columbia University Press, 1978.

Brown, Cedric C., ed. *Patronage, Politics, and Literary Tradition in England, 1558–1658*. Detroit, Mich.: Wayne State University Press, 1993.

Bush, Douglas. *Prefaces to Renaissance Literature*. New York: W. W. Norton, 1965.

Buxton, John. *Elizabethan Taste*. London: Harvester, 1963.

Cowan, Alexander. *Urban Europe, 1500–1700*. New York: Oxford University Press, 1998.

Driver, Tom E. *The Sense of History in Greek and Shakespearean Drama*. New York: Columbia University Press, 1960.

Finucci, Valeria, and Regina Schwartz, eds. *Desire in the Renaissance: Psychoanalysis and Literature*. Princeton, N.J.: Princeton University Press, 1994.

Fumerton, Patricia, and Simon Hunt, eds. *Renaissance Culture and the Everyday*. Philadelphia: University of Pennsylvania Press, 1999.

Halliday, F. E. *Shakespeare in His Age*. South Brunswick, N.J.: Yoseloff, 1965.

Harrison, G. B., ed. *The Elizabethan Journals: Being a Record of Those Things Most Talked of During the Years 1591–1597*. Abridged ed. 2 vols. New York: Doubleday Anchor, 1965.

Harrison, William. *The Description of England: The Classic Contemporary [1577] Account of Tudor Social Life.* Edited by Georges Edelen. Washington, D.C.: Folger Shakespeare Library, 1968. Reprint, New York: Dover, 1994.

Jardine, Lisa. "Introduction." In Jardine, *Reading Shakespeare Historically.* London: Routledge, 1996.

————. *Worldly Goods: A New History of the Renaissance.* London: Macmillan, 1996.

Jeanneret, Michel. *A Feast of Words: Banquets and Table Talk in the Renaissance.* Translated by Jeremy Whiteley and Emma Hughes. Chicago: University of Chicago Press, 1991.

Kernan, Alvin. *Shakespeare, the King's Playwright: Theater in the Stuart Court, 1603–1613.* New Haven: Yale University Press, 1995.

Lockyer, Roger. *Tudor and Stuart Britain, 1471–1714.* London: Longmans, 1964.

Norwich, John Julius. *Shakespeare's Kings: The Great Plays and the History of England in the Middle Ages, 1337–1485.* New York: Scribner, 2000.

Pollard, A. J. *Richard III and the Princes in the Tower.* Godalming, UK: Bramley Books, 1997.

Rose, Mary Beth, ed. *Renaissance Drama as Cultural History: Essays from Renaissance Drama, 1977–1987.* Evanston, Ill.: Northwestern University Press, 1990.

Ross, Charles. *Richard III.* Berkeley: University of California Press, 1983.

Saccio, Peter. *Shakespeare's English Kings.* 2nd ed. Oxford: Oxford University Press, 1997.

Schmidgall, Gary. *Shakespeare and the Courtly Aesthetic.* Berkeley: University of California Press, 1981.

Smith, G. Gregory, ed. *Elizabethan Critical Essays.* 2 vols. Oxford: Clarendon Press, 1904.

Tillyard, E. M. W. *The Elizabethan World Picture.* London: Chatto and Windus, 1943. Reprint, Harmondsworth: Penguin, 1963.

Willey, Basil. *The Seventeenth Century Background: Studies in the Thought of the Age in Relation to Poetry and Religion.* New York: Columbia University Press, 1933. Reprint, New York: Doubleday, 1955.

Wilson, F. P. *The Plague in Shakespeare's London*. 2d ed. Oxford: Oxford University Press, 1963.

Wilson, John Dover. *Life in Shakespeare's England: A Book of Elizabethan Prose*. 2d ed. Cambridge: Cambridge University Press, 1913. Reprint, Harmondsworth: Penguin, 1944.

Zimmerman, Susan, and Ronald F. E. Weissman, eds. *Urban Life in the Renaissance*. Newark: University of Delaware Press, 1989.

Dramatic Development

Cohen, Walter. *Drama of a Nation: Public Theater in Renaissance England and Spain*. Ithaca, N.Y.: Cornell University Press, 1985.

Dessen, Alan C. *Shakespeare and the Late Moral Plays*. Lincoln: University of Nebraska Press, 1986.

Fraser, Russell A., and Norman Rabkin, eds. *Drama of the English Renaissance*. 2 vols. Upper Saddle River, N.J.: Prentice Hall, 1976.

Happé, Peter, ed. *Tudor Interludes*. Harmondsworth: Penguin, 1972.

Laroque, François. *Shakespeare's Festive World: Elizabethan Seasonal Entertainment and the Professional Stage*. Translated by Janet Lloyd. Cambridge: Cambridge University Press, 1991.

Norland, Howard B. *Drama in Early Tudor Britain, 1485–1558*. Lincoln: University of Nebraska Press, 1995.

Theater and Stage

Doran, Madeleine. *Endeavors of Art: A Study of Form in Elizabethan Drama*. Milwaukee: University of Wisconsin Press, 1954.

Grene, David. *The Actor in History: Studies in Shakespearean Stage Poetry*. University Park: Pennsylvania State University Press, 1988.

Gurr, Andrew. *Playgoing in Shakespeare's London*. Cambridge: Cambridge University Press, 1987.

———. *The Shakespearian Stage, 1574–1642*. 3d ed. Cambridge: Cambridge University Press, 1992.

Halliday, F. E. *A Shakespeare Companion, 1564–1964*. Rev. ed. Harmondsworth: Penguin, 1964.

Harrison, G. B. *Elizabethan Plays and Players*. Ann Arbor: University of Michigan Press, 1956.

Holmes, Martin. *Shakespeare and His Players.* New York: Scribner, 1972.

Ingram, William. *The Business of Playing: The Beginnings of the Adult Professional Theater in Elizabethan London.* Ithaca, N.Y.: Cornell University Press, 1992.

Lamb, Charles. *The Complete Works and Letters of Charles Lamb.* Edited by Saxe Commins. New York: Modern Library, 1935.

LeWinter, Oswald, ed. *Shakespeare in Europe.* Cleveland, Ohio: Meridian, 1963.

Orgel, Stephen. *The Authentic Shakespeare, and Other Problems of the Early Modern Stage.* New York: Routledge, 2002.

Ornstein, Robert. *A Kingdom for a Stage: The Achievement of Shakespeare's History Plays.* Cambridge, Mass.: Harvard University Press, 1972.

Salgado, Gamini. *Eyewitnesses of Shakespeare: First Hand Accounts of Performances, 1590–1890.* New York: Barnes and Noble, 1975.

Stern, Tiffany. *Rehearsal from Shakespeare to Sheridan.* Oxford: Clarendon Press, 2000.

Thomson, Peter. *Shakespeare's Professional Career.* Cambridge: Cambridge University Press, 1992.

Webster, Margaret. *Shakespeare without Tears.* New York: Whittlesey House, 1942.

Weimann, Robert. *Shakespeare and the Popular Tradition in the Theater: Studies in the Social Dimension of Dramatic Form and Function.* Edited by Robert Schwartz. Baltimore: Johns Hopkins University Press, 1978.

Wikander, Matthew H. *The Play of Truth and State: Historical Drama from Shakespeare to Brecht.* Baltimore: Johns Hopkins University Press, 1986.

Yachnin, Paul. *Stage-Wrights: Shakespeare, Jonson, Middleton, and the Making of Theatrical Value.* Philadelphia: University of Pennsylvania Press, 1997.

Biography

Halliday, F. E. *The Life of Shakespeare.* Rev. ed. London: Duckworth, 1964.

Honigmann, F. A. J. *Shakespeare: The "Lost Years."* 2d ed. Manchester: Manchester University Press, 1998.

Schoenbaum, Samuel. *Shakespeare's Lives.* New ed. Oxford: Clarendon Press, 1991.

———. *William Shakespeare: A Compact Documentary Life.* Oxford: Oxford University Press, 1977.

General

Bergeron, David M., and Geraldo U. de Sousa. *Shakespeare: A Study and Research Guide.* 3d ed. Lawrence: University of Kansas Press, 1995.

Berryman, John. *Berryman's Shakespeare.* Edited by John Haffenden. Preface by Robert Giroux. New York: Farrar, Straus and Giroux, 1999.

Bradby, Anne, ed. *Shakespearian Criticism, 1919–35.* London: Oxford University Press, 1936.

Colie, Rosalie L. *Shakespeare's Living Art.* Princeton, N.J.: Princeton University Press, 1974.

Dean, Leonard F., ed. *Shakespeare: Modern Essays in Criticism.* Rev. ed. New York: Oxford University Press, 1967.

Feiling, Keith. *A History of England.* New York: McGraw-Hill, 1948.

Goddard, Harold C. *The Meaning of Shakespeare.* 2 vols. Chicago: University of Chicago Press, 1951.

Kaufmann, Ralph J. *Elizabethan Drama: Modern Essays in Criticism.* New York: Oxford University Press, 1961.

McDonald, Russ. *The Bedford Companion to Shakespeare: An Introduction with Documents.* Boston: Bedford, 1996.

Raffel, Burton. *How to Read a Poem.* New York: Meridian, 1984.

Ricks, Christopher, ed. *English Drama to 1710.* Rev. ed. Harmondsworth: Sphere, 1987.

Siegel, Paul N., ed. *His Infinite Variety: Major Shakespearean Criticism Since Johnson.* Philadelphia: Lippincott, 1964.

Sweeting, Elizabeth J. *Early Tudor Criticism: Linguistic and Literary.* Oxford: Blackwell, 1940.

Van Doren, Mark. *Shakespeare.* New York: Holt, 1939.

Weiss, Theodore. *The Breath of Clowns and Kings: Shakespeare's Early Comedies and Histories.* New York: Atheneum, 1971.

Wells, Stanley, ed. *The Cambridge Companion to Shakespeare Studies.* Cambridge, Cambridge University Press, 1986.

FINDING LIST

Repeated unfamiliar words and meanings, alphabetically arranged, with act, scene, and footnote number of first occurrence, in the spelling (form) of that first occurrence

abides	4.2.22	*battle* (noun)	1.3.81
abortive	1.2.19	*bedashed*	1.2.104
abroad	1.1.130	*befall*	1.3.157
account (noun)	3.2.18	*beholding*	2.1.63
advance (verb)	1.2.36	*belike*	1.1.63
advancement	1.3.43	*bend* (verb)	1.2.76
advantage	3.5.28	*betide*	1.2.17
afford	1.2.146	*black*	1.2.31
alarums	1.1.13	*blemish* (verb)	1.2.94
anon	1.4.68	*blunt* (adjective)	1.3.63
argues	3.7.13	*boon*	1.2.131
arms	1.1.11	*borne*	1.3.62
aspect	1.2.21	*bottled*	1.3.135
attend	1.2.134	*brave* (verb)	4.3.24
bark (noun)	3.7.47	*brooked*	1.1.125
basilisks	1.2.100	*bunchbacked*	1.3.137

shallow	2.2.2	*touch* (noun)	1.2.59
signify	1.4.50	*touches* (verb)	1.1.116
slave (noun)	1.2.73	*toys*	1.1.70
smoothing	1.2.107	*triumphant*	3.2.24
soft	1.3.182	*true*	1.1.49
sort (verb)	2.2.51	*ungoverned*	2.2.41
sound (verb)	3.1.65	*unquiet*	2.4.23
speed (verb)	2.3.4	*untainted*	3.1.4
spleen	2.4.27	*untimely*	1.2.4
spurn	1.2.38	*vassals*	1.4.72
state	1.3.70	*villain*	1.1.43
stay (verb)	1.2.30	*vouchsafe*	1.2.61
stir	1.3.178	*want* (verb)	1.1.26
stopped in	1.4.20	*warrant* (noun)	1.3.185
straight	1.3.194	*way*	1.1.84
straitly	1.1.93	*wayward*	1.3.13
subtle	1.1.50	*we*	1.1.2
successively	3.1.31	*well-advised*	1.3.171
sudden	1.3.187	*wherefore*	1.4.69
suit	1.2.138	*whet* (verb)	1.3.136
ta'en (taken)	4.1.20	*withal*	1.1.106
take (verb)	3.5.41	*witness* (verb)	1.3.151
tardy	2.1.42	*wits*	1.2.85
tedious	1.4.47	*wonderful*	1.2.60
tender (adjective)	3.1.8	*worthy*	1.2.71
tender (verb)	2.4.32	*would*	1.2.97
thrive	2.1.8	*wrangling*	1.3.90
timorously	3.5.24	*yield* (verb)	1.3.97